This book on getting more ⟨...⟩ helpful book of all R. T. Ke⟨...⟩ R. T. has taken a subject most people would never give much attention to and made it into a most inviting read. My reasons for believing it may be his best are:

- It is intensely *practical*, dealing with a long list of issues and problems in life and ministry that really need to be addressed.

- It is up close and *personal*! R. T. has dared to show us here his deepest secrets, some I've never heard him share before.

- Forgive the alliteration, but another word fits here: this book is *poignant*; that is, it causes slight feelings of pain as the author dares to reveal past hurts. At other times it elicits deep regrets over our own past hurts.

To sum it up, I would say, "Read his book! It will encourage you, caution you, and challenge you to genuinely want more of God!"

Thanks, R. T. You've done it again!

—JACK TAYLOR
DIMENSIONS MINISTRIES

This book is a passionate cry from the heart of someone who knows that going deeper with God means honoring His Word and hungering for His Spirit. R. T.'s teaching is wise and winsome, but above all it has been proved through a lifetime's experience of walking with the Lord.

—PAUL HARCOURT
NATIONAL LEADER, NEW WINE

In this masterful work, *More of God*, R. T. Kendall reorganizes our spiritual priorities by challenging and encouraging believers to pursue God for who He is and not just for what He can do. This book will take you further and deeper into a living experience with the one and true God.

—Dr. Tony Evans
President, The Urban Alternative
Senior Pastor, Oak Cliff Bible Fellowship

The Word and the Spirit bring us to the same truth: there is nothing in life that we need more than God, and nothing we need to experience more of more than God. In this Spirit-guided book R. T. Kendall invites us to hunger and thirst for what matters most, for God and His kingdom. Jesus promises the Holy Spirit to those who ask Him; let us take Him at His word and always welcome more of what God will do in our lives. It is not sufficient to know about God; God invites us to know Him, to know and enjoy His heart, to live our lives in the light of His presence, to depend on Him.

—Craig Keener
Professor of New Testament, Asbury Theological
Seminary, Wilmore, Kentucky

I think *More of God* may be my favorite R. T. Kendall book! From the earliest days of my walk with God, I have focused on getting more of God. I wish I'd had this book fifty years ago to help me understand that there is a huge difference between receiving more *from* God and embracing more *of* God Himself. I encourage you to get alone with this book for a few days and let the Spirit do the same work in you that He has done in me!

—Stephen Chitty
Pastor, Christian Life Church
Columbia, South Carolina

# MORE
## *of*
# GOD

R.T. KENDALL

CHARISMA
HOUSE

Most CHARISMA HOUSE BOOK GROUP products are available at special quantity discounts for bulk purchase for sales promotions, premiums, fund-raising, and educational needs. For details, write Charisma House Book Group, 600 Rinehart Road, Lake Mary, Florida 32746, or telephone (407) 333-0600.

MORE OF GOD by R. T. Kendall
Published by Charisma House
Charisma Media/Charisma House Book Group
600 Rinehart Road
Lake Mary, Florida 32746
www.charismahouse.com

Visit the author's website at rtkendallministries.com.

Library of Congress Cataloging-in-Publication Data:
An application to register this book for cataloging has been
submitted to the Library of Congress.
International Standard Book Number: 978-1-62999-584-7
E-book ISBN: 978-1-62999-585-4

This publication is translated in Spanish under the title *Más
de Dios*, copyright © 2019 by R. T. Kendall, published by Casa
Creación, a Charisma Media company. All rights reserved.

While the author has made every effort to provide accurate
internet addresses at the time of publication, neither the
publisher nor the author assumes any responsibility for errors or
for changes that occur after publication. Further, the publisher
does not have any control over and does not assume any
responsibility for author or third-party websites or their content.

19 20 21 22 23 — 987654321
Printed in the United States of America

*To*
*Roger, Josh, and Ricky*

*I pray ... that you may be filled to the measure of all the fullness of God.*
—EPHESIANS 3:17, 19, NIV

# CONTENTS

# FOREWORD

AFTER READING MORE than forty books written by Dr. R. T. Kendall, I think I have found my favorite one. Through his writings I've learned to forgive, handle trials, pray, worship, walk in my anointing, not grieve the Holy Spirit, live for His praise only and in the light of the final judgment, and so much more. With each book I've been amazed that the Holy Spirit gave R. T. so much insight.

With this book it becomes clear that so many of the insights in prior books were preparing his readers step by step to come to this place—to receive *more of God*. R. T. quotes A. W. Tozer as saying that we can have as much of God as we want. My experience has been that it always requires us to let go of the things of lesser value that would hinder us or take His place.

The Holy Spirit is drawing many to pursue God in a fresh way in this season. We long to see a revival in our nation and renewal in the church. Are you experiencing this drawing? Everything in this book is designed to make you hungrier and to show the path to receiving more of Him. God is *real* and has made Himself available to us!

—Joy Strang
CFO, Charisma Media

# FOREWORD

I HAVE JUST FINISHED reading a most helpful and digestible manuscript of wise words. This book has an easy flow that is beautifully written and carries the reader onward to the next wonderful chapter. The reader senses he or she is being mentored by an experienced onetime pastor and popular traveling speaker.

This book is a compendium of helpful counsel being gently whispered in one's ear—no condemnation, just encouragement. The book contains frequent references to Scripture and keeps the Lord at the center in each chapter.

R. T. illustrates some of the common mistakes Christians make with frank disclosures of his own experience to drive home the point being made. The book challenges many misleading interpretations or misunderstandings of the Word and some of our faulty practices.

I first heard R. T. leading some Bible readings at a conference—New Wine, an annual gathering of many thousands mainly made up of church parties from across Britain. This manuscript appears to sum up the best of all his many books.

I hope it finds its way across the world. I was sorry when I reached the end, as it left me feeling I had been basking in the presence of the Lord for what seemed a nice long quiet time. I recommend it to Christians everywhere. God bless them all.

—DAVID PYTCHES
FORMER ANGLICAN BISHOP IN CHILE (1958–1977)
FORMER LEADER, ST. ANDREW'S CHURCH, CHORLEYWOOD,
HERTS, ENGLAND

# FOREWORD

THE LORD SPOKE to me recently and said, "I love the world!" Well, that got my attention. "For God so loved the world…" (John 3:16). I knew that verse well, but the Lord went on to say, "They know they're lost, and they know they need Me. I wish My church knew the same thing. They could have all of Me if they wanted Me, but they have all of Me that they want." How much more of God do you want?

I really felt a sense of sadness come over me, but not for me—I felt sad for the Lord. He didn't say that with a happy tone in His voice. Revelation 7:17 says, "And God will wipe away every tear from their eyes." I'm sure that's true, but maybe He's wiped away everybody's tears but His own.

The Lord also said, "The seeker-friendly message that the church has been preaching is producing more tares than wheat." He wasn't too happy about that one either. I really think it breaks His heart when we take the word of someone else over His Word. The psalmist said He esteems His Word higher than His name (Ps. 138:2). So if His name is above every name, then how much more does He truly honor His own Word?

Many of our churches today want more people more than they want more of God. The Holy Spirit can't be controlled, and control is something few people are willing to give up. Our lives are too busy, too complicated to have more of God. It's just one more thing to have to deal with. Are we willing to give up our time to have more of God?

We preach just enough of the Bible to keep the older generation sitting comfortably on their blessed assurance, and then comes the self-help message—five easy steps to becoming a better (fill in the blank)—the kind of sermon that doesn't offend visitors or the new members. Brothers and sisters, if we could get saved reading a self-help book, then our precious Savior died for no reason. The blood of Jesus, the forgiveness of our sins, and the power of the Word of God are the only things in heaven or on earth that can save us, change us, mold us, and make us into vessels of honor, fit for the Master's use (2 Tim. 2:21).

It's rare these days to hear a message on the power of the resurrection, the power of the blood of Jesus, the power that's in His name, or the mighty power and blessing of praying in the Holy Spirit! "But you, beloved, building yourselves up in your most holy faith and praying in the

Holy Spirit…" (Jude 20). The very thing that God sent us as a gift at Pentecost—on the day the church was born with such unity of heart—is the very thing that the devil has used for two thousand years to divide the church: the gift of speaking in tongues. If the Lord sent it to 120 people knowing how much they were going to need it at that time, then how much more do we need that gift now? Lord, we need more of Your Holy Spirit! Baptize us with the Holy Ghost and fire!

We live in a society where bigger is better, where more people joining the church is necessary just to keep the lights on, pay the rent on the building, and pay for the new sound system or sports complex. There is nothing wrong with having all those things, but when those things have us, that's when we compromise. Jesus said, "Seek first the kingdom of God and his righteousness, and all these things will be added to you" (Matt. 6:33).

There are usually two opinions that I'm faced with every day—my opinion and God's opinion. I've come to realize that He doesn't care very much for my opinion; His opinion is the only one that matters. He's already ruled on it. "For ever, O Lord, thy word is settled in heaven" (Ps. 119:89, kjv). His most holy and infallible Word cannot be changed, only fulfilled. Here again, do we take Him at His Word, or do we take the word of someone else? God is looking for someone who will agree with Him. If you want more of God in your life, start agreeing with His Word. That's a great first step! There is such power in agreement. It's who we agree with that matters to the Lord. Think about the Garden of Eden and how quickly Adam and Eve were deceived. They agreed with the wrong voice. After hearing the voice of God from the time of creation, how quickly they were deceived. The Lord Jesus told His disciples, "Take heed that you not be deceived" (Luke 21:8, NKJV).

John the Baptist said, "He must increase, but I must decrease" (John 3:30), and I totally believe that's true. I've seen it in my own life. It's the laying aside of our will, our reputation, our status in society, our position on the rung of the ladder of success, our ministries, our friends, our families, our jobs—whatever is keeping us from pressing in to having more of God. Because no matter how much of God any of us has right now, there is a hundred times more of Him to be had. We have not because we ask not. We ask not because we want not! Do we really want more of His power and presence in our lives? Are we willing to go bankrupt of self to have more of God?

> Enoch walked faithfully with God; then he was no
> more, because God took him away.
> —GENESIS 5:24, NIV

I believe that Enoch had such a hunger for God and such a life of communion with the Father that there was no more of Enoch to be had. The Lord just consumed him. That was an Old Testament event, and we have a better covenant on this side of the cross. "Behold, I stand at the door and knock. If anyone hears My voice and opens the door, I will come in to him and dine with him, and he with Me" (Rev. 3:20, NKJV).

I was looking at the famous Warner Sallman painting

of Jesus standing and knocking at the door, and a friend of mine said to me, "See anything unusual about the door?"

I looked for a while and then I saw it. I said, "Yes, it doesn't have a handle on the outside."

He said "That's right. The only way that door will open is from the inside."

If we don't want to invite the Lord to come in, then He won't. He only comes where He's invited. Are we willing to open the door of our heart to the King of kings? What an honor to have Him come and visit us. We would open the door for anyone else we knew; why would we not open up for Jesus? Maybe because our house is a little messy, or there might be some things lying around that we would be ashamed for the Lord to see, as if He doesn't see them anyway. "Where is my Bible? I know it's in here somewhere." God is sending us an invitation for a visitation. Right now while you're reading this, will you let Him in? One word from the Lord is greater than a million words from men!

> My sheep hear My voice, and I know them, and they follow me.
>
> —JOHN 10:27

Is it possible in this day and time to be so consumed by the presence of the Lord that there is none of us left, only the Lord? I believe it is possible. "With God all things are possible" (Mark 10:27, KJV).

I believe the Lord Jesus gave His life for us so that we could have the same kind of relationship with the Father that He had. I can tell you, I'm not there.

Jesus, His presence, His nature, His life, His spirit, His love, His mercy, His forgiveness, His gentleness, His patience, His kindness, His boldness for the sake of the gospel, His heart for the lost, His jealousy for His Word, His jealousy for His people, and His jealousy for His glory—these are the things worth fighting for. These are the things that can help us to have more of God. These things are focused on the Lord and His nature. When the world sees us demonstrating these things, walking them out in our everyday lives, and living intentionally Christlike in everything we say or do, then the lost will want to be found. Don't you want more of God? I sure do. I need more of Him and less of me in my life.

R. T. Kendall has been writing books that are so right for the times we're in. And this book, *More of God*, is right on time as well. I heard a prophetic friend of mine say, "God is coming to us before He comes for us." I believe that is so true. He wants to come to us and fill us, not just with His Spirit inside when we get saved but also with the tangible presence of God on the outside. This is the thing that causes the atmosphere to change around us. When He shows up, things change! When He shows up, the devil is nowhere to be found. That's a good thing.

I believe that Joel 2:28 has yet to be fulfilled. On the day of Pentecost, when the Lord poured out His Spirit in the upper room, Peter said, "This is that which was spoken by the prophet Joel" (Acts 2:16, KJV). And he went on and quoted the Joel scripture: "I will pour out my Spirit on all flesh" (v. 17). Everyone that was in that room definitely got hammered by the Holy Ghost! But the scripture says *all flesh*—not just 120 saved people, praying and fasting for the promise of the Helper, the Holy Ghost. I believe with my whole heart that the Word of God means what it says and says what it means. And the Word says *all flesh*. Now that says to me that there are people who are not saved who will be getting an outpouring of the Holy Spirit when God decides to fulfill that scripture. It's His Spirit; He will pour it out on all flesh when He wants to, and we'd better not argue with the Lord about who is and isn't worthy of His Spirit. It seems to me that the Lord is getting His church ready to receive these newly filled and newly saved people—sons, daughters, women servants, and men servants—all flesh.

Now, will everyone receive His Spirit? I don't know that. Two thieves on the cross—one received His love and found forgiveness and a place in paradise, while the other blasphemed Him to His face and wouldn't receive the free gift of pardon. It's the condition of the heart. Many in the church are facing the same question; which one will we be? Will we humble ourselves and find grace and mercy, knowing we can do nothing to gain our salvation, or will we turn away from Him like the other thief? I do know that we've got to be ready to minister love to these people when they ask, "What the heck just happened to me?" It will be like cleaning fish. It will be messy, and it will stink! But the joy that's in heaven even when one person comes to the Lord Jesus is worth it all to Him. "In the same way, I tell you, there is rejoicing in the presence of the angels of God over one sinner who repents" (Luke 15:10, NIV). That's why we need more of God. It's not just for us; it's for the harvest. Revival is coming! This will be the church's finest hour. Some people think that the church's greatest days have come and gone. That's what the devil wants you to think, but Jesus called him "the father of lies" (John 8:44).

Do we want more of God or more from God? I think He has been a patient, long-suffering God to put up with us the way He has. You know with all that is in you that the things of this world are changing. We as Christian believers are being attacked for our faith, not just in foreign countries but right here in our own backyard. But the Lord is using every bit of these attacks to strengthen us for the battles ahead. He's not doing this to us; He's doing this for us, for our own good, for the good of the kingdom.

Let's go for more and more of God. He wants it more than we do. He loves the journey with us. I think He misses people like Enoch and Adam and Eve—ones who walked with Him and had relationship with Him. He's not a lonely God, but He is a God who loves being alone—alone with us!

—RICKY SKAGGS

# PREFACE

I'VE WRITTEN THIS book for the Christian. Whereas it will certainly do you no harm if you are not a Christian, I have written this for those who have been justified by faith in the blood of Jesus Christ. My assumption, therefore, is that you, the reader, are saved: your sins are forgiven, and you have transferred your trust in good works to what Jesus has done for you on the cross. You know that you will go to heaven when you die.

With that in mind I have sought to show in this book how you can get more of God.

I dedicate this book to members of my board—Roger Perry, Josh Hankins, and Ricky Skaggs—all residents of Hendersonville, Tennessee. God has been very gracious to Louise, T. R., and me in giving us such people to help govern my ministry.

I am pleased that Ricky Skaggs has written an amazing foreword to this book. He is the most unusual person in show business that I know of—unashamed of the gospel, unashamed of Jesus of Christ. Winner of fourteen Grammys, Ricky has been inducted into both the Country Music Hall of Fame and the Gospel Music Hall of Fame. I warmly welcome his sharing his heart as he has.

I also welcome Bishop David Pytches of Great Britain's foreword, which was prepared for British readers.

My thanks as always to Steve and Joy Strang of Charisma House for publishing this book and especially to Debbie Marrie, my editor, for her wisdom. But my deepest debt is to Louise—my best friend and critic.

—R. T. KENDALL
MAY 2018

# Chapter 1

# MORE *FROM* GOD OR
# MORE *OF* GOD?

*I the* LORD *your God am a jealous God.*
—EXODUS 20:5

D O YOU WANT more *of* God, or do you want more *from* God?

If you are like many people in the church today, you want more *from* God more than you want more *of* God. Wanting more *of* God is desiring Him for what He is in Himself. Paul prayed that the Ephesians would "be filled with all the fullness of God" (Eph. 3:19). Wanting more *from* God is *using* Him to accomplish your goals. Wanting more *of* God is partaking of the "divine nature, having

1

escaped from the corruption that is in the world because of sinful desire" (2 Pet. 1:4). Wanting more *from* God is seeking Him to get what you want. In his sermon "Your God vs. the Bible's God," Rolfe Barnard (1904–1969) stated that most people today use God "like a farmer uses a milk cow"—using Him for what they can get without regard to who He is.[1]

There is a fine line between wanting more *of* God and wanting more *from* God. The two can easily overlap. What is more, if I pray for more *of* God, I am in fact asking for more *from* God; namely, that I might get more *of* Him *from* Him. Not only that, "The heart is deceitful above all things, and desperately sick; who can understand it?" (Jer. 17:9). It is not so easy to get to the bottom of our true motives. *Why* do I want more *of* God? Is it so I can get more *from* Him? What will more *of* God do for me? Why would I want more *of* God? Or *should* I want more *of* God?

With these questions asked, I want to make the case in this book that wanting more *from* God may be very different from wanting more *of* Him.

- Wanting more *of* Him means you want Him for His own sake; wanting more *from* Him means you want certain things that He might give you.

- Wanting more *of* Him is focusing on what He is like; wanting more *from* Him is focusing on what He can do for you.

- Getting more *of* Him is knowing His Word better and having more of His Spirit; getting more *from* Him is using Him to achieve your goals.

- Getting more *of* Him is getting to know who He is; getting more *from* Him is focusing on yourself.

- Getting more *of* Him is dignifying His will; getting more *from* Him is dignifying your agenda.

I remember querying the wisdom of an old friend—Lynn Green—many years ago for going to a church to get prayed for when the Toronto Blessing (as people called it) was beginning to flourish. His kind reply put me in my place: "I want all of God I can get." I never forgot that. I thought, "A desire like that cannot be wrong." I began to ask myself whether I wanted more of God so much that I would be willing to swallow my pride and go wherever I might get more of God.

I then asked: "Do I really want more of God? And do I want all of God I can get?" A.W. Tozer (1897–1963) said that we could have as much of God as we want! I have pondered that statement for many years.

## THE CRUCIAL QUESTION

Can we really have as much of God as we want? Good question. But it is not the most important question. The crucial question is, What does God Himself want for us?

What does He want us to want? Does He Himself want us to have more *of* Him, or does He encourage us to request more things *from* Him? Or is more *of* Him given to us mainly so we can meet our personal needs, wishes, and goals? What if our goals are not consistent with His plans for us?

The question comes down to this: Why has God revealed Himself to us? It is, of course, primarily to save us and assure us that we will go to heaven when we die. But there is more. Every Christian is called to come into his inheritance. Some do; some don't. Whether we come into our inheritance can be put in terms of whether we want more *of* God or more *from* God.

## FOUNDATION AND SUPERSTRUCTURE

Assurance of salvation is the foundation for getting to know God. Being on that foundation means we can then build a superstructure. The quality of our superstructure will determine our reward at the judgment seat of Christ (2 Cor. 5:10). As we shall see in more detail, Paul uses metaphors to show that the quality of one's superstructure is based on the building materials (1 Cor. 3:12). The superstructure comprised of gold, silver, and precious stones—which survives the fire of judgment—is determined by whether we want more *of* God. The superstructure made of wood, hay, and straw—which burns up in the fire of judgment—comes by merely wanting more *from* God.

Since God has revealed Himself to us, He wants us to know Him as He is in Himself—and wants us to want more *of* Him. That is what this book is about.

There are, however, those who teach that God exists for us mainly to *use* Him. Such teaching is highly appealing. It often motivates people like no other. It appeals to our fleshly nature. Sadly many good people are consequently never taught to consider the possibility that God has revealed Himself to us so that we *might know Him as He is*—apart from doing things for us. Such thinking is hardly on their radar screen. Therefore, the premise that God is there that we might know Him and have more of Him—apart from doing things for us—is alien to some.

## "Name It and Claim It"

A few years ago Louise and I considered moving from Hendersonville, Tennessee, into downtown Nashville, Tennessee. We found a lovely condo apartment and so wanted to live there. But there were obstacles.

To help us overcome the obstacles, a well-meaning Christian lady insisted that we go to the very building and pray. "If you want this apartment, you can have it. *Claim it as yours* in the name of the Lord," she said confidently. She volunteered to go with us. "Let's go to the building itself and pray there—and you will get it," she promised.

I was not comfortable with this line of thinking, but, partly wanting to please this sincere lady and partly hoping that perhaps I was being stubborn and missing something that her theology offered us, we went to the ground floor of the building. She prayed, and we prayed with her, claiming the promise "if two of you agree on earth about anything they ask, it will be done for them by my Father in heaven" (Matt. 18:19). It turned out that someone else got this beautiful apartment a day or so later, and we gave up our wish to move for the time being.

This lady was somewhat typical of those who hold to a "name it and claim it" theology, also known as "believe it and receive it" type of thinking. These phrases are fairly apt descriptions of certain teaching that suggests you can have almost anything you want from God. Name it—a better job, a new car, healing—then claim it. Believe it is yours, and you will get it.

This "prosperity gospel," as some call it, attracts many people, and they travel for miles to attend annual conferences to hear this teaching expounded, based upon selected scriptures. As a result a lot of pastors—including certain television preachers—have made this their central focus and base this teaching on their interpretation of the Bible.

It often comes down to this: money and material possessions. God wants you to have these things, say these preachers. Some see this perspective in almost every verse in the Bible and even claim it as the main reason Jesus died for us. You can understand why this teaching is appealing.

The lady who prayed with Louise and me has been well taught. Her pastor greatly admires her. She is also highly intelligent—being a professor at a well-known university in Nashville—and she was adamant that God would give us that apartment.

## WHAT'S IN IT FOR GOD?

The "What's in it for me?" age has become the warp and woof of many in the church today. The question "What's in it for God?" hardly ever comes up. People don't seem to care what's in it for God. The very idea has not crossed their minds. Who cares?

I do. That is why I have written this book.

When God gave the Ten Commandments to the children of Israel on Mount Sinai 3,400 years ago, He identified Himself as a "jealous" God. He actually said, "I the LORD *your* God am a jealous God" (Exod. 20:5, emphasis added). The God who spoke like that was Israel's God. That means He is *our* God. All of us are "the Israel of God" (Gal. 6:16). As surely as you have received Jesus Christ as your Lord and Savior, the God of the Bible is *your* God. You belong to Him. And He loves you with a jealous care. I love it. Some people hate it. Why would they hate it? Is it not fantastic that almighty God loves us that much?

It also means, however, that He wants His will for us to be respected, honored, obeyed, and accomplished in us. God loves every person as though there were no one else to love, said Saint Augustine (354–430), and has plans for each of us as if there were no one else He has plans for.[2]

To put it another way, God has an opinion on everything. Ponder that for a moment. God has an opinion on everything. The trouble is, we don't always want His opinion! We are afraid it might be different from ours! True wisdom is to get God's opinion—and follow it to the hilt.

*Doxa,* the Greek root word for *glory,* means opinion. God's jealousy is also His glory. Glory is the total of all His attributes. His glory is His opinion. According to Paul, we are "predestined according to the purpose of him who works all things according to the counsel of his will...to the praise of his *glory*" (Eph. 1:11–12, emphasis added).

God wants us to *know* Him. According to Jesus, eternal life is knowing God. He said to His Father—who is our Father: "And this is eternal life, that they know you, the only true God, and Jesus Christ whom you have sent" (John 17:3).

Some think God mainly wants us to *use* Him. There is a place for this. Of course there is. We shall see this clearly in this book. But it must *follow* getting to know God.

We must first get acquainted with the God of the Bible and esteem knowing Him more than we desire riches and personal glory. Some people introduce others to God on the basis that He wants us mainly to use Him to get what we want. Sadly they have bypassed the heart of God and are incalculably impoverished.

To know God is to affirm Him for being just like He is—including that He is a jealous God. So when we pray for more of God, we gladly accept Him as He is. It invariably means accepting not only His Word and His ways but also His will. "Therefore do not be foolish, but understand what the will of the Lord is" (Eph. 5:17).

Essential to knowing the God of the Bible is embracing the fact that He has a will of His own. It is not our task to change His will; it is our mandate to find out what His will is and accomplish it. Those who approach God mainly to change His will—even if they don't mean to— show disrespect for His sovereignty. They want to change His will because they assume they have a better idea than God has.

God has a will of His own. For each of us. A plan. He is not looking to us for input. His Word—the Holy Scriptures—reveal His will. It is an unimprovable will. What He has in mind is infinitely better than anything we can come up with. You cannot improve on what He already has in mind. "For the LORD God is a sun and shield; the LORD bestows favor and honor. No good thing does he withhold from those whose walk uprightly" (Ps. 84:11). In a word, God only wants what is best for us. We are fools if we try to "upgrade" what God has in mind.

## GNOSTICISM

The ancient Gnostics were among the first major enemies of the true gospel of Jesus Christ. The word *gnostic* comes from the Greek *gnosis* (knowledge). The Gnostics proposed a new way of knowing. It was dangerous teaching.

They wormed their way into the church (Jude 4). Their presence was like a cancer in the body of Christ. They flattered Christians, praising them for the good things they believed. But they told the Christians they would make their faith even better and that they should listen to them. Wherever they succeeded, the Christian faith was compromised and eventually disappeared. It is the devil's ploy.

The Gnostics in fact hated the true God and His Son, Jesus Christ. Their promise to make the Christian faith "better" was a lie from the pit of hell. The truth is, the Christian faith "once for all delivered to the saints" (Jude 3) is unimprovable. It is perfect.

So too is God's will. Those who try to improve on it

are deceived and will deceive you too. God's will is good, pleasing, and perfect (Rom. 12:2). Don't try to improve on it; accept it. Adjust to it. This is true wisdom.

> Get wisdom; get insight; do not forget, and do not turn away from the words of my mouth. Do not forsake her, and she will keep you; love her, and she will guard you. The beginning of wisdom is this: Get wisdom, and whatever you get, get insight. Prize her highly, and she will exalt you; she will honor you if you embrace her. She will place on your head a graceful garland; she will bestow on you a beautiful crown.
>
> —PROVERBS 4:5–9

Wisdom has nothing to do with a person's IQ, culture, breeding, or education. It is within reach of all of us. It begins with the fear of the Lord (Prov. 1:7; 9:10). It's as simple as that. If you and I will fear God, we will avoid a lot of trouble down the road. If we will fear the Lord more than we fear man, which is a snare (Prov. 29:25), we will obtain true wisdom. We will have no regrets in life. We will not miss what God has in mind for us.

That said, do note these words: "though it cost all you have, get understanding" (Prov. 4:7, NIV). Whatever does that mean? Do we have to pay for it with money? That would mean the wealthy can get it quickly, but you and I may never get it! Good news! It does not cost us money. In that sense it is free.

But it does have a cost. It costs our pride and our reputation. It means sometimes having to look ridiculous, resisting temptation, abandoning personal plans, and giving up friendships and associations that are not God honoring. But the cost is worth it. The garland of grace on our heads is worth it all. It comes to all who esteem God's will above the praise of people.

Getting wisdom—getting more of God—costs everything, and yet it's free.

> Come, everyone who thirsts, come to the waters; and he who has no money, come, buy and eat! Come, buy wine and milk without money and without price. Why do you spend your money for that which is not bread, and your labor for that which does not satisfy? Listen diligently to me, and eat what is good, and delight yourselves in rich food. Incline your ear, and come to me; hear, that your soul may live; and I will make with you an everlasting covenant, my steadfast, sure love for David. Behold, I made him a witness to the peoples, a leader and commander for the peoples. Behold, you shall call a nation that you do not know, and a nation that did not know you shall run to you, because of the LORD your God, and of the Holy One of Israel, for he has glorified you.
>
> —ISAIAH 55:1–5

A few years ago I was reading my Bible on a plane from New York to Miami, Florida. When my eyes fell on the words of Moses in Exodus 33:13, a verse I have read countless times, I was sobered from head to toe. The funny thing is, it was a request to get something *from* God! And what do you suppose it was?

> If I have found favor in your sight, please show me now your ways, that I may know you in order to find favor in your sight.
>
> —EXODUS 33:13

Here is the background. God had let Moses know that He was pleased with Moses. The implication was that Moses was now in a bargaining position with God—that if God was pleased with him, Moses could now ask for anything and get it. And what was it that Moses asked for? Riches? Long life? Judgment upon his enemies? Personal glory or vindication? None of these. His request: "show me now your ways." That is what he asked for—to know God's ways.

We all have our ways. My wife knows my ways; I know her ways. My close friends know my ways. They may not admire all my ways, but these behaviors and habits mirror who I am.

God has ways. Like them or hate them, He has His ways. God is who He is, and His ways will not change (Mal. 3:6). His ways reflect Him as He is in Himself—His person, His character, His attributes. God lamented of ancient Israel: "They have not known my ways" (Ps. 95:10; Heb. 3:10). God wanted Israel to know His ways.

- When Moses was in a position to ask God for anything, he requested to know God's ways.

- When Solomon was invited to ask for
  anything, he chose wisdom (1 Kings 3:9;
  2 Chron. 1:10). God was pleased with this
  request.

After I had read Exodus 33:13 and also thought of Solomon's request, I began asking different people, "If you could ask anything from God and knew you would get it and God would not hold it against you no matter what the request was, what would you ask for?" I got answers such as good health, long life, and to win the lottery. One replied, "That my daughter would come back to the Lord"—a godly request.

What would you ask for if you could have anything?

When Jesus could ask for anything, He prayed for you and me. We saw that He revealed what eternal life is— namely, that we would know the true God and His Son, Jesus Christ (John 17:3). Jesus has actually prayed for you and me. Our being Christians is a direct answer to His prayer in John 17. He wants us to know His Father and to know Jesus Christ Himself.

Paul's deepest longing was this: "I want to know Christ—yes, to know the power of his resurrection and participation in his sufferings, becoming like him in his death" (Phil. 3:10, NIV). That is Paul's way of saying he wants more of God.

It is therefore the will of our Lord Jesus Christ that we know God. He wants you and me to know His ways. He wants us to *want* to know His ways. This means He wants

13

us to want more of Him. This also means He is willing to grant us more of Him.

Why was I sobered when I read Exodus 33:13 as if for the first time? It was because I had not asked for this myself. I have asked for other things, and perhaps they were not so bad—such as wanting a double anointing. But asking for a double anointing can be so selfish and self-serving. But when I saw what Moses wanted—and saw the person Moses was and the person God used—I felt utterly ashamed. I am ashamed now to admit that up until then it had not crossed my mind to ask to know God's ways. I realized how little I knew God and began to pray that somehow God might make up for the previous fifty years or so I had not prayed like that.

Was it too late to get to know God's ways? I asked. I hope not. For this is what I still ask for now.

I am making a big issue of seeking more *of* God rather than seeking more *from* Him. If after all that I've written, you still pray to receive more *from* Him, glory to God. The issue is receiving from Him what is pleasing to Him—never forgetting that He is a jealous God.

*More of God* is the title of this book because I hope it will appeal to people who genuinely want more of God. And I earnestly pray it will make you hungry for more of God and lead you to get more of God.

Those who hear me preach will know that I almost always begin a sermon with a prayer that the Holy Spirit will sprinkle those present with the blood of Jesus. I want to be as sure as I can that those who listen will receive what I say without any misunderstanding or misinterpretation and that I will be clear and simple. You might like to know that I also pray daily that the Holy Spirit will sprinkle the minds of all the readers of my books with the blood of Jesus. I trust therefore that God is answering my prayer for you as you read this book. I seek to be simple and clear. I so want you to want more of God and get more of God.

# Chapter 2

# MORE *ABOUT* GOD OR
# MORE *OF* GOD?

*How much more will the heavenly Father give
the Holy Spirit to those who ask him!*
—Luke 11:13

I KNOW IT SEEMS unfair to say this, but having more of God is, for me, impossible to describe in such a way that anyone can truly grasp. One can certainly try, of course, and I somewhat attempted to do this in my book *The Presence of God.* But describing objectively what may take place subjectively—when it comes to more of God Himself—is beyond the level of my ability to write. God is greater than anything we can say about Him. His presence is more awesome than anything we can say about it. In other words, words fail.

You may ask, "Why write about it if *more of God* cannot be described?" I answer, "I want this book to make you hungry." That is my purpose. God's Word creates a hunger and thirst for more of Him. If I am true to His Word in this book, the result will be (1) you have a hunger and thirst *in you* as you read; (2) you will eventually experience for yourself how real God is. You have this promise from Jesus: "Blessed are those who hunger and thirst for righteousness, for they will be filled" (Matt. 5:6, NIV). That means you will be satisfied. No one needs to tell you if the water you drank when you were thirsty made you feel better. So too with experiencing God—and more of God.

That is all I want to come from your reading this book—for you to experience God for yourself. When that happens, you will know it for yourself. You won't have to ask, "Am I now experiencing more of God?" As long as you have to ask that, you have not yet experienced Him for yourself.

> But what to those who find? Ah, this
> Nor tongue nor pen can show;
> The love of Jesus, what it is,
> None but His loved ones know.[1]
> —BERNARD OF CLAIRVAUX (1091–1153)

No sign in northwest Arizona says "*This* is the Grand Canyon." There are no signs in Switzerland that say "You are now looking at the Swiss Alps." I will never forget the first time I saw them. I was in awe. No photo or painting of them exactly portrays what they are like and how they make you feel. You need to be there and see them firsthand. It is like being hot, sweaty, and thirsty on a humid August day—and then you start drinking cold water. No one has to tell you how you feel at that moment!

Having more of God is like that.

It is the point of all the books in the Bible. God gave us the thirty-nine books of the Old Testament and the twenty-seven books of the New Testament that we might experience God Himself. Of the twenty-seven books of the New Testament, all were written that one might get more of God—not merely know more *about* Him but experience *Him*.

That said, it is important to know more about Him. I love the hymn "More About Jesus."

> More about Jesus would I know,
> More of His grace to others show;
> More of His saving fullness see,
> More of His love who died for me.[2]
> —ELIZA E. HEWITT (1851–1920)

I want to know more and more about Jesus—not with the view of passing on new information or with the motive of using such knowledge; I want to know what Jesus is like. Just to know Him. To feel Him. To recognize Him. To hear Him speak, no matter what He has to say. Whatever comes from His lips is good enough for me. It is like Mary sitting at the feet of Jesus.

Now as they went on their way, Jesus entered a village.
And a woman named Martha welcomed him into
her house. And she had a sister called Mary, who sat
at the Lord's feet and listened to his teaching. But
Martha was distracted with much serving. And she
went up to him and said, "Lord, do you not care that
my sister has left me to serve alone? Tell her then
to help me." But the Lord answered her, "Martha,
Martha, you are anxious and troubled about many
things, but one thing is necessary. Mary has chosen
the good portion, which will not be taken away
from her."

—LUKE 10:38–42

Many years ago we were visiting a Baptist church in
Moscow. I wondered what the difference was between
Christians in Russia and those in the United States. The
pastor made a shrewd observation, comparing Eastern
Christianity with Western Christianity. "We in the East
are more like Mary, sitting at the feet of Jesus, while you
in America are like Martha, distracted by many things."

That said, I suggest this book—possibly written more
for Christians in the West—might lead us to be more like
those Russians I just described. Mind you, those were the
days of the Soviet Union when I suspect Christians probably spent more time depending on God than perhaps is
the case today.

My point is this: we can probably *learn more about
God* more easily than we can *find more of God.* For
example, reading books—including my own—may come
more easily than doing nothing but praying and reading

your Bible. Of course I would like to think that this book you are now reading would lead you to get more of God. But this will only happen if the hunger and thirst for Him drive you to your knees.

I think of the lines from two well-known hymns, both written by the same English woman.

> I love to tell the story, for those who know it best
> Seem hungering and thirsting to hear it like the rest.[3]
> —A. KATHERINE HANKEY (1834–1911)

> Tell me the story slowly,
> That I may take it in,
> That wonderful redemption,
> God's remedy for sin.
> Tell me the story often,
> For I forget so soon;
> The early dew of morning
> Has passed away at noon.[4]
> —A. KATHERINE HANKEY

The difference between knowing more *about* God and knowing more *of* God is the difference between experiencing something secondhand and experiencing it firsthand. Knowing about God is information—which is very important. But that is not enough. You need more—but not just more information.

I used to debate with a friend who said, "You get it all when you are initially converted. There's no more available," he argued. "The next thing after conversion is heaven." He based his argument on Paul's word that our being in Christ means "you are not lacking in any gift, as you wait for the revealing of our Lord Jesus Christ" (1 Cor. 1:7).

But he missed the point Paul made later in the same epistle, having given a list of spiritual gifts. "Earnestly desire the higher gifts," he said, and then he promised to show them the "more excellent way" (1 Cor. 12:31). That more excellent way is the love described in 1 Corinthians 13. Not all have the gifts, says Paul, but we can covet them and ask God for them. Neither is the experience of 1 Corinthians automatic; it is something to be pursued. We must experience it firsthand.

It is thrilling to hear stories of people who have had firsthand experiences with God. It is wonderful to hear stories that come out of great revivals, whether the Cane Ridge Revival or the Welsh Revival. They can inspire us. They can even make us hungry! But such stories are still secondhand.

Theology, for example, is secondhand information about God. We learn it in Bible schools, divinity schools, and seminaries. Sound theology is essential, but if theology—even if it is sound, solid, and substantial—is all you get, you have come short of getting more *of* God. Getting more of God cannot be yours by mere teaching; getting more of Him is what must *happen* to you. The best I can do—short of that happening to you—is to *point the way.*

Knowing more *about* God and knowing more *of* Him is the difference between head knowledge and heart knowledge. Head knowledge is important. Paul pointed out that "now you wholeheartedly obey this teaching we have given you" (Rom. 6:17, NLT). However, had that teaching been understood in mind only, no obedience would have followed. Head knowledge is never enough. They obeyed the teaching because it made its way to the *heart*.

> If you confess with your mouth that Jesus is Lord and believe in your heart that God raised him from the dead, you will be saved. For with the heart one believes and is justified, and with the mouth one confesses and is saved.
>
> —ROMANS 10:9–10

The difference between head knowledge and heart knowledge is the difference between mental assent to the truth and *persuasion* of the truth. In the Middle Ages *faith* was defined as mental assent to the teaching of the church. Christians at that time may or may not have known what the church taught, but they would say, "If the church teaches it, I believe it." They could remain ignorant that way.

Ignorance might be bliss to some, but when you are *persuaded* of a teaching, it means you have not only grasped it mentally but embraced it in your heart. It is because you have become convinced. The Greek word for *faith* is *pistis*; this comes from the root word *peitho*, which means persuasion. If you are not persuaded, you are no better off.

The seat of saving faith is the heart. It is when head knowledge drops into the heart. "The penny drops," Brits would say, this being the belated realization of something after a period of confusion or ignorance. "The longest journey you will ever take," said British politician Andrew

Bennett, "is the eighteen inches from your head to your heart."[5] But this is true of all of us.

It is true of saving faith. The heart must be involved. When Peter preached on the day of Pentecost, his hearers were "cut to the heart" (Acts 2:37). He was able to preach like that because he had more of God than he had before the falling of the Holy Spirit on the day of Pentecost. He knew a lot about God after hearing Jesus speak countless times over the previous three years. Such knowledge about God did not keep him from denying the Lord three times (John 18:17, 25–27). But after the coming of the Spirit, Peter was a different man.

Therefore, the heart must be engaged after conversion. All teaching about more of God will be merely theological if it stimulates only the mind.

This book is about moving beyond saving faith. It is about getting more of God, experiencing more of God. This is why I mentioned the books of the New Testament earlier; they are written that we might get more of God. Take the letters. Those addressed were already saved, but the writers wanted them to experience not just more knowledge *about* God—of which the letters are full to overflowing—but more *of* God. For example, here are exhortations that show there is more:

- "Do not be conformed to this world, but be
  transformed by the renewal of your mind,
  that by testing you may discern what is the
  will of God, what is good and acceptable
  and perfect" (Rom. 12:2).

- "Run in such a way as to get the prize" (1 Cor. 9:24, NIV).

- "I feel a divine jealousy for you, since I betrothed you to one husband, to present you as a pure virgin to Christ" (2 Cor. 11:2).

- "My little children, for whom I am again in the anguish of childbirth until Christ is formed in you" (Gal. 4:19).

- "That you may be filled with all the fullness of God" (Eph. 3:19).

- "And this is my prayer that your love may abound more and more, with knowledge and all discernment" (Phil. 1:9).

- "That you may stand mature and fully assured in all the will of God" (Col. 4:12).

- "May the God of peace himself sanctify you completely" (1 Thess. 5:23).

- "That you may obtain the glory of our Lord Jesus Christ" (2 Thess. 2:14).

- "The aim of our charge is love that issues from a pure heart and a good conscience and a sincere faith" (1 Tim. 1:5).

- "For God has not given us a spirit of fear and timidity, but of power, love, and self-discipline" (2 Tim. 1:7, NLT).

- "To further the faith of God's elect and their knowledge of the truth that leads to godliness" (Titus 1:1, NIV).

- "I pray that the sharing of your faith may become effective for the full knowledge of every good thing that is in us for the sake of Christ" (Philem. 6).

- "You have need of endurance, so that when you have done the will of God you may receive what is promised" (Heb. 10:36).

- "That you may be perfect and complete, lacking in nothing" (Jas. 1:4).

- "But the God of all grace, who hath called us unto his eternal glory by Christ Jesus, after that ye have suffered a while, make you perfect, stablish, strengthen, settle you" (1 Pet. 5:10, KJV).

- "He has granted to us his precious and very great promises, so that through them you may become partakers of the divine nature, having escaped from the corruption that is in the world because of sinful desire" (2 Pet. 1:4).

- "If we walk in the light, as he is in the light, we have fellowship with one another, and the blood of Jesus his Son cleanses us from all sin" (1 John 1:7).

- "Watch yourselves, so that you may not lose what we have worked for, but may win a full reward" (2 John 8).

- "But you, beloved, building yourselves up in your most holy faith and praying in the Holy Spirit" (Jude 20).

- "Let the one who is thirsty come; let the one who desires take the water of life without price" (Rev. 22:17).

Are you thirsty for more of God? That thirst came from Him. "Delight yourself in the LORD, and he will give you the desires of your heart" (Ps. 37:4). He would not put that desire in your heart to tease you, to tantalize you, to get your hopes up, and to give you this hunger for Him were He not going to keep His promise—that you will be filled.

All that follows in this book is designed to make you hungry. Thirsty. As you read, keep in mind that the ever-increasing hunger for more of God is from God. The devil would not put that desire there. The flesh would not put that desire there. Only God can do that!

There is a difference between knowing about God and knowing God. Dr. Martyn Lloyd-Jones (1899–1981) used to say that so many books he read on knowing God should have been titled *Knowing About God*. You can know about someone and not know the person. You can become an expert on the Grand Canyon without going there. You can become an expert on the historic revivals in the Christian church without ever experiencing revival. I fear that much of the theology taught nowadays is information from those who do not know God. They only know about God.

Pharaoh spoke the truth when he said, "I do not know the LORD" (Exod. 5:2). I'm afraid there are those who have professed faith in Christ but do not know Him. They walked forward in an evangelistic meeting, signed a card, and—perhaps—joined a church and got baptized but still do not know the Lord.

Do you know the Lord? You cannot pursue more of Him until you know Him. But if you are hungry and thirsty for righteousness, this is a solid indication that you know Him—or you would not have a desire like that! Be encouraged. More than that, if you are hungry and thirsty for righteousness, congratulations! The best translation of the Greek word *makarios*—translated "blessed" in the Beatitudes in most versions of the Bible—is "congratulations."[6] Oh yes! When you have a desire like that, it is a wonderful sign that God is on you. It means God is on your case. Be congratulated when this is true.

My advice: don't settle for more mere information about God or more theological knowledge. Don't settle for cerebral stimulation about divine things. Give yourself no rest until you cross over the crucial line from second-hand knowledge about God to firsthand knowledge of God. And when you come into this realm, you will be conscious of how real the God of the Bible is. He is real. More real than the air you breathe, more real than nature you see. There is nothing more exciting than when you see for yourself that God is real, Jesus is real, the Holy Spirit is real, and the Bible is true!

27

Is that what you want? Congratulations! Is that would you long for? You will be filled. And you will not need anyone to tell you that you have experienced more of God. You will know for yourself. You might even feel like the queen of Sheba when she said to Solomon:

> The report was true that I heard in my own land
> of your words and of your wisdom, but I did not
> believe the reports until I came and my own eyes
> had seen it. And behold, the half was not told me.
> —1 KINGS 10:6–7

Jesus spoke graciously to a woman of Samaria. She then reported her time with Him to the town. They later said to the woman, "It is no longer because of what you said that we believe, for we have *heard for ourselves*, and we know that this is indeed the Savior of the world" (John 4:42, emphasis added).

I cannot adequately describe what getting more of God is. But as surely as your hunger and thirst for more of God increase, you will come to know more of God for yourself. It is more wonderful than drinking sweet, cool water when you are thirsty on a hot summer day.

> And I tell you, ask, and it will be given to you; seek,
> and you will find; knock, and it will be opened to
> you. For everyone who asks receives, and the one
> who seeks finds, and to the one who knocks it will
> be opened. What father among you, if his son asks
> for a fish, will instead of a fish give him a serpent;
> or if he asks for an egg, will give him a scorpion? If

you then, who are evil, know how to give good gifts
to your children, how much more will the heavenly
Father give the Holy Spirit to those who ask him!

—LUKE 11:9–13

# Chapter 3

# OUR NEVER-CHANGING PRIORITY

*But seek first the kingdom of God and his righteousness,
and all these things will be added to you.*
—MATTHEW 6:33

MATTHEW 6:33 WAS my father's favorite verse in the Bible. He must have quoted it to me at least a hundred times as I grew up. It is a wonderful verse and so relevant to this book.

Why is Matthew 6:33 so important? It appears in the second half of Jesus' famous Sermon on the Mount, and it shows what is *invariably* the next step forward when it comes to our needs and wants. It is true twenty-four hours a day, seven days a week. We never outgrow seeking the kingdom of God *first*—before we pursue anything else.

That said, there are other priorities we must examine in this chapter. What else does the Bible tell us to seek?

## How to Approach the Throne of Grace

Let's start with mercy. According to Hebrews 4:16—written to Hebrew Christians—the first thing we should ask for in prayer is not grace to help us in time of need but mercy:

> Let us then with confidence draw near to the throne
> of grace, that we may receive mercy and find grace
> to help in time of need.

God has sought to protect the throne of grace from people like you and me by requiring we ask for mercy first, as opposed to rushing into God's presence demanding this or that. Too many of us approach God and lay our wants and wishes before Him without ever thinking of who He is or His honor. Because we know He is a loving and caring God, we tend to rush into His presence and begin to ask for this and that without any thought to the character of God. But Hebrews 4:16 instructs us to ask for mercy first. You might say: "Surely not; that is what we ask for in order to receive salvation! After all, an integral part of conversion is to pray, 'God, be merciful to me, a sinner' (Luke 18:13)." True. But whatever made you think you outgrow asking God for mercy? The writer addresses Hebrews 4:16 to Christians!

Let the holiest and most godly reader of this book

understand this: you never outgrow the need to ask God for mercy. No matter how long you have been a Christian (I converted when I was six years old—that was seventy-seven years ago), you must ask God for mercy before you begin putting your requests to Him.

- Have you been on a forty-day fast recently? Do you feel prayed up and confident in your relationship with God? Wonderful! You must ask for mercy before you outline your needs to the Lord.

- Are you experiencing victory over a habit that has plagued you for years? Good! But you still need to ask for mercy first when approaching the throne of grace.

- Have you resisted sexual temptation, forgiven your enemy, or been praying for an hour a day, or do you have a Bible reading plan that takes you through the Word in a year? These things are excellent. But you never outgrow needing to ask for mercy when you approach God.

- Do you attend church regularly, curb your hours of watching television, and spend more time reading godly books? Splendid. You still must ask for mercy when you pray.

- Have you been worshipping God by singing your favorite worship song again and again?

I'm glad to hear it. You still must humbly
ask God for mercy when you turn to Him.

Are your prayers not getting answered? We have all
experienced this. But has it crossed your mind that maybe
God is not answering your prayers for a reason? Part of
the reason could be that your requests are ill-posed; that
is, you are asking for something that is not God's will for
you. After all, God hears us when we ask according to His
will (1 John 5:14). But the reason could also be that you are
merely *using* God when you pray because you only pray
when you want something.

The throne of grace presupposes some sovereign sits on
that throne. Yes, it is King Jesus. A sovereign has the right
to invite who comes into his presence. When my British
friends enter the presence of their monarch, they bow or
curtsy. How much more when we approach the throne of
grace? We ask for mercy.

A very prominent Anglican clergyman said to Louise
and me that virtually one hundred out of one hundred
people who come to him want something from him. How
many go to a man like that just to bless him, pray for him,
and encourage him? Virtually no one.

Traveling preacher Arthur Blessitt once told me that
many years ago he asked Pope John Paul, "What can I do
for you?" The pope was rather startled and said to him,
"Nobody ever asks me that. They all want something from
me." People would approach Billy Graham (1918–2018)
for the same reason—or a member of the royal family, a

member of parliament, a US senator, a congressman, or the president.

The preceding paragraph mentions people. Human beings. Important? Yes. But they are people. They need our prayers.

God doesn't need our prayers. And yet He wants us to pray—not because He needs us but because we need Him.

However, God, being a jealous God, wants our worship and our praise. He wants to have His will carried out in our lives. He wants us to affirm Him for who He is: the one and only true God, sovereign of the universe, the Maker of heaven and earth.

## THE FEAR OF GOD

I have reason to believe that the fear of God is coming back to the church. The fear of God has been absent for a long, long time. You might say: "Surely the fear of God is Old Testament teaching." Really? On the island of Patmos, John had a vision of an angel announcing the "eternal gospel." In a loud voice he said, "Fear God and give him glory" (Rev. 14:6–7). "Fear came upon every soul" immediately after the Spirit of God fell on the day of Pentecost (Acts 2:43, MEV).

When Peter began his sermon on the day of Pentecost, the people scoffed at the 120 filled with the Holy Spirit (Acts 2:13). But they were not making fun when Peter finished preaching. The fear of God fell on the people. They were "cut to the heart" and asked, "What shall we do?" (Acts 2:37).

The most notable sermon ever preached in America

was on July 8, 1741, when Jonathan Edwards (1703–1758) preached his sermon "Sinners in the Hands of an Angry God." Taking his text from Deuteronomy 32:35, "Their foot shall slide in due time" (KJV), Edwards read his sermon word for word. People said he had a poor delivery. But the Spirit of God came down on the people as he spoke: "The God that holds you over the pit of hell, much as one holds a spider...it is nothing but His hand that holds you from falling into the fire every moment."[1] People began to groan and weep. By the time he finished, they were literally clutching the backs of church pews to keep from sliding into hell. Men were seen holding on to tree trunks outside to keep from sliding into hell. It was a mere taste of judgment to come. God only did it once. News of this sermon spread all over New England in days. It spread all over England in weeks. It was the high-water mark of the Great Awakening (1726–1750).

A restoration of the gospel of Christ and the fear of God will result in people crying to God, asking for mercy. Try this: begin your prayer by asking for mercy. Did you realize that God can give or withhold mercy, and justice would be done either way? This should keep us humble. This should keep you and me from snapping our fingers at God and expecting Him to jump. Never forget what He said to Moses only moments after Moses prayed to know God's ways: "I will have mercy on whom I will have mercy, and I will have compassion on whom I will have compassion" (Exod. 33:19, NIV). God is sovereign. And lest you say, "But that's Old Testament teaching," I remind you that Paul quoted this in Romans 9:15. God's sovereignty is as inherent in His character and attributes as His jealousy. It is the essence of the glory of God—His opinion.

You may ask, "Must I literally use the word *mercy* every time I pray?" Probably not. But your frame of mind and the attitude of your heart should show an awareness that God does not have to answer your prayers. He is God. He is in the heavens; He does whatever He pleases (Ps. 115:3).

Take a look at the healing of the leper in Matthew chapter 8. In Jesus' day a leper could not live among the rest of society. Back then leprosy was an untreatable disease and feared to be highly contagious. A leper in Judaism had to wear torn clothes, let his hair be unkempt, cover the lower part of his face, and cry out, "Unclean, unclean" (Lev. 13:45). The leper in Matthew 8 knew better than to snap his fingers at Jesus and demand to be healed; instead, he came to Jesus on bended knee and said, "Lord, if you will, you can make me clean" (v. 2). It was tantamount to saying, "Lord, I know You don't have to heal me, but if You are willing, I know You can make me clean." Jesus said, "I am willing…be clean" (v. 3, NIV).

We should all imitate the leper when we pray.

God is rich in mercy (Eph. 2:4). He loves to grant mercy—especially when we specifically ask for it. It honors Him. It shows dignity and respect for who He is.

## THE LORD'S PRAYER

Consider the Lord's Prayer. In Luke's account the disciples told Jesus, "Lord, teach us to pray" (Luke 11:1), and Jesus responded with a prayer that teaches *how* to pray. It is a pattern prayer, also a prayer to be prayed. My wife,

Louise, and I pray it together literally every day. Notice how it begins.

> Our Father in heaven, hallowed be your name.
> —MATTHEW 6:9

The first thing we should pray for—according to this— is that God's name will be hallowed throughout the world. We should pray that God will be famous. The Beatles' John Lennon boasted years ago that they were "more popular than Jesus."[2] Sadly true. We should pray that God will again be famous in the world. Praying "hallowed be your name" shows God's priority for us when we pray.

In my book *The Lord's Prayer* I seek to make the case that God has His prayer list—and puts His list first. He puts three requests: (1) that we pray for His holy name to be honored; (2) that we pray for His kingdom to come to us; and (3) that we pray for His will to be done as perfectly on earth as perfectly it is being carried out in heaven. That's His prayer list for us. That said, Jesus added a prayer list for each of us to pray: (1) "give us this day our daily bread" (Matt. 6:11); (2) "forgive us our debts, as we also have forgiven our debtors" (v. 12); (3) "lead us not into temptation" (v. 13); and (4) "deliver us from the evil one" (v. 13, NIV).

Does it surprise you that God puts His prayer list first? The fact that the Lord would put His prayer list first is a strong hint that we should honor *Him* and *His will* before we put our requests to Him. After all, He is a jealous God.

This should teach us to approach God with the deepest respect. Instead of focusing on our agenda, we begin by focusing on His. He wants us to pause and recognize that we are talking to God Almighty, the Creator of heaven and earth.

Admittedly there are times—in a sudden and painful crisis—we may well cry out or even scream, "God!" We've all done this. God is absolutely fine with it. But even then at the bottom of our hearts there should be an awareness that God can give or withhold mercy. The Lord's Prayer—the pattern for how we should pray—shows us the proper attitude to have when we pray.

## THE KINGDOM OF GOD

When Jesus brought in this crucial verse—"Seek first the kingdom of God and his righteousness"—these words *followed* His exposition of the Mosaic Law in the Sermon on the Mount. It is impossible to know how much His original hearers grasped of this teaching at first. Until the Holy Spirit came down on the day of Pentecost, they assumed that the kingdom of God was not only earthly but accompanied by the overthrow of Rome—putting Israel back on the map. Jesus stated clearly that the kingdom of God does not come by observation; it is "within you" (Luke 17:20–21, KJV). They still didn't get it, even asking after Jesus was raised from the dead if He would not restore the kingdom to Israel (Acts 1:6). I think, therefore, that it is unlikely that people grasped His Sermon on the Mount with much depth. What we do know is that they marveled that He spoke with "authority," unlike the teachers of the Law (Matt. 7:28–29)

Michael Eaton (1942–2017) thought Jesus took at least

two or three days to preach this, that what we have in Matthew 5–7 is a summary of His sermon. My book *Sermon on the Mount* is a verse-by-verse exposition of this sermon. The kingdom of God is the theme. I, therefore, want now to give a summary of what Jesus taught about the kingdom of God in the Sermon on the Mount. It will help us to know what Jesus meant by seeking first the kingdom of God.

The Sermon on the Mount is Jesus' doctrine of the Holy Spirit. The whole sermon will make complete sense when one sees this. The kingdom of heaven is the realm of the Holy Spirit, with Jesus being the King. To dwell in the kingdom of heaven is to be filled with the ungrieved Holy Spirit. It means the Holy Spirit must be in us ungrieved, unquenched. It is possible to grieve the Holy Spirit (Eph. 4:30) or quench the Holy Spirit (1 Thess. 5:19). But when the Holy Spirit in us is utterly Himself—that is, not grieved by our fleshly anger—we will be able to *surpass* the righteousness of the Pharisees and teachers of the Law.

Jesus said two things about keeping the Mosaic Law. First, He said He would fulfill it (Matt. 5:17). According to Dr. Martyn Lloyd-Jones, this is the most stupendous statement Jesus ever made—that Jesus Himself would fulfill the Law. It was a promise to do something never done before; namely, keep the Law to the hilt—the moral law (the Ten Commandments), the ceremonial law (how God should be worshipped), and the civil law (how the people of Israel should govern themselves). When Jesus died on the cross, it was mission accomplished! When He said, "It is finished" (John 19:30), it was a statement of victory—that Jesus did exactly what He said He would do. For that reason, said Paul, our faith in Jesus' blood imputes righteousness to us. The righteousness of Jesus—namely, His sinless life and sacrificial death—is put to our credit by faith alone, faith plus nothing (Rom. 3:25–4:5).

The second thing Jesus said regarding keeping the Law was this: unless our righteousness exceeds or "surpasses" the righteousness of the Pharisees, we could not enter the kingdom of heaven. Since the Pharisees were seen as outwardly impeccable, however, could any human being exceed their righteousness? Since they tithed, must we double-tithe? Since they fasted twice a week, must we fast three times a week? No. The Pharisees did not realize that they kept the Law outwardly but not inwardly. They did not murder people, and they did not sleep with other men's wives; therefore, they thought themselves to have been without sin.

Jesus then came up with the astonishing word—never heard before; namely, that hating, holding a grudge, and unforgiveness were tantamount to murder (Matt. 5:21–22). Lusting after a woman—or causing her to lust—was adultery in the heart (vv. 27–28). The way, therefore, that one surpassed the outward righteousness of the Pharisees was by forgiving and blessing one's enemy and stopping lusting or causing a woman to lust.

Jesus dealt with only three of the Ten Commandments: the sixth (do not murder), the seventh (do not commit adultery), and the third (do not misuse the name of the Lord). Jesus elaborated on the command not to murder when He said, "Love your enemies and pray for those who persecute you" (v. 44). He elaborated on the third commandment when He said, "Do not swear an oath at all" (v. 34, NIV). Swearing by heaven or earth or Jerusalem was misusing the name of the Lord.

Surpassing the righteousness of the Pharisees means there is to be no hate, no lust, and no misuse of the name of the Lord. When we do not forgive, when we lust, or when we misuse the name of God, we grieve the Holy Spirit. Inhabiting the kingdom of God, therefore, means that the ungrieved Spirit reigns in our hearts. This is basically what Jesus meant by entering the kingdom of God.

What does it mean to seek *first* the kingdom of God? In a word, it means to seek God's agenda before we focus on our needs. It is not easy to do this; we naturally want to put ourselves first. But it's how God wants us to live: putting His agenda before our personal needs. In Matthew 6:33 Jesus assumes that His hearers—and we may rightly assume His readers too—have not forgotten what He has been teaching about the kingdom of God. The kingdom of God is the realm of the Holy Spirit; entering it is having the ungrieved Spirit dwelling in our lives. The Holy Spirit is a very sensitive person, as I show in my book *The Sensitivity of the Spirit*. For example, when we hold a grudge or engage in sexual lust, it grieves Him.

Embracing the kingdom of God, therefore, means that we put into practice what Jesus preached. Doing this results in an acute awareness of sin and the need to exceed the righteousness of the Pharisees. The Pharisees had no awareness of sin. They were utterly self-righteous. As I said, they thought they kept the Law because they did not kill anybody and because they did not physically sleep with another man's wife. The way one surpasses the righteousness of the Pharisees, then, is by understanding Jesus' interpretation of the Mosaic Law. We are going to see this in more detail to follow. In short it meant not hating in your heart, not lusting in your heart, and not misusing the name of the Lord (Matt. 5:21–37). This is why the Sermon on the Mount cannot be truly understood until you see that it is our Lord's doctrine of the Holy Spirit. It means we must embrace *His* interpretation of the Law and how it is fulfilled in us. It means having an acute awareness of sin and a bent of life toward not grieving the Holy Spirit. Therefore, to seek first the kingdom of God and His righteousness means that we prioritize our relationship with God and His Spirit versus seeking to get our needs and wants supplied.

This shows the difference between seeking more *of* God and seeking more *from* God. Seeking the kingdom of God *first* is seeking more *of* God.

Jesus taught that we should never worry. We should not worry about life or what we eat or drink. We should not worry about the body or what we wear. This section of the Sermon on the Mount followed His reference to money. We should store up for ourselves treasures in heaven not treasures on earth. We cannot serve both God and money. That is when He brought in His teaching about worry and physical needs such as food, shelter, and clothing.

> So do not worry, saying, "What shall we eat?" or "What shall we drink?" or "What shall we wear?"

> For the pagans run after all these things, and your
> heavenly Father knows that you need them. But
> seek first his kingdom and his righteousness, and
> all these things will be given to you as well.
> —MATTHEW 6:31–33, NIV

I don't mean to be unfair, but it seems to me that the "name it and claim it" teaching I referred to previously encourages one to focus on the very things that Jesus said pagans seek after! I think we should run as far away from that way of thinking as we possibly can!

I urge you to seek first the kingdom of God—the rule of the ungrieved Spirit—and His righteousness, the righteousness that exceeds the righteousness of the scribes and Pharisees. If you want more of God, this is the way forward.

Seeking the kingdom of God first, then, means putting holiness before anything else. It is the pursuit of a life that does not grieve the Holy Spirit. It is the pursuit of a life in which the ungrieved Spirit dwells.

What follows? According to Jesus, "all these things will be added to you." What things? Food, shelter, clothing—the essentials of life, what we need. You may recall that the first petition on our prayer list in the Lord's Prayer is, "Give us this day our daily bread." That is a petition that covers our basic needs—food to eat, clothes to wear, a place to live, sleep, and good health. Physical needs and emotional needs. These things are "added," or "given," to us when we get our priorities right.

But when we make food, shelter, and clothes our priority,

we violate this glorious promise in Matthew 6:33. These things are a *given*, says Jesus. Don't worry about these things. God will take care of these things. He feeds the sparrow. God makes the lilies grow. He looks after nature. We pray for our daily bread, yes, but we don't worry about having daily bread. God assures us that this is His problem; He has put His integrity on the line to look after the essentials of our lives.

Seeking more of God, then, is seeking first the kingdom of God. To have more of God is to have increased inner strength to resist sexual temptation; it is to have an unfeigned love by which we bless and pray for our enemies. Seeking more than the essentials of life—seeking more from God—is going beyond what God has promised. He promised to supply all our needs according to His riches in glory (Phil. 4:19). When we seek more from God—driving a Mercedes, staying in a five-star hotel, living in luxury and splendor—we try to outdo Him.

Don't do that. "Godliness with contentment is great gain" (1 Tim. 6:6). "Keep your life free from love of money, and be content with what you have, for he has said, 'I will never leave you nor forsake you'" (Heb. 13:5).

By the way, God may give you a Mercedes. Don't count on it, but He might do it. He has done it for some! But I must be as honest as I know how to be with you: if you start seeking things like that, you are going beyond wanting more *of* God to wanting more *from* God.

Question: Which do you want—more *from* God or more *of* God? If you sincerely seek more *of* God and He gives you things that exceed what you ask or think, good!

But make your aim to seek more *of* Him—what honors Him, what will not grieve the Holy Spirit, what will enable you to know His ways, and what will give you great *peace*. This is what Jesus means by seeking *first* His kingdom *and* righteousness—namely, the righteousness that surpasses that of the Pharisees. It means you truly honor the Sermon on the Mount and grasp what He meant by the kingdom.

This is the way God wants us to live.

# Chapter 4

# ACCEPTING OUR LIMITATIONS

*For by the grace given to me I say to everyone among*
*you not to think of himself more highly than he ought*
*to think, but to think with sober judgment, each*
*according to the measure of faith that God has assigned.*
—ROMANS 12:3

I HAVE ONE GIFT," Billy Graham said to me. "It's giving an appeal"—that is, giving an invitation for people to come forward at the close of his sermon. I think that is a modest assessment. He always insisted that he was not a great preacher. I disagree. It is my view that he was a great preacher. There are those who have said that Billy Graham was a creation of the press. If there is some truth to this, did not God use the media to exalt him? And yet who among us would not welcome almost any channel, person, or organization that might use our ministry more widely? Part of one's anointing is *connected* to the doors God sovereignly opens and those He strategically closes. In other words, one's anointing is not limited to one's talent; how it reaches the world is equally a part of one's anointing. Opening and closing doors—this is what God does.

One of my closest friends at Trevecca Nazarene College (now University) in the 1950s was Paul Hilton (not his real name). He was possibly the most brilliant person I ever met. Proficient in several languages, Paul was also at home with theology, literature, mathematics, and physics. He was, I would have to say, very godly. But he was not in demand. He wept openly to me one day because he feared that "the world will not discover my gift." He was an introvert, quite boring to be with—I was possibly his only friend—and he did not appear to have the makings of a preacher. A few years later he went right into the world and refused to keep in touch with me. He died without any renewal of repentance, as far as I know.

I have thought a lot about Paul over the last sixty years. Why would God give such an ingenious mind to the church without giving him a corresponding place of usefulness? Trying to find the answer is, strange as it might seem to you, walking on "holy ground." That is my phrase for what God does not permit us to know. It is like Moses noticing that the burning bush was not consumed. He decided to investigate. "I will go over and see this strange sight—why the bush does not burn up." God told him to *stop*! "Do not come near; take your sandals off your feet, for the place on which you are standing is holy ground" (Exod. 3:5). Moses tried to figure out what was happening. He was not allowed to get any closer. It was holy ground.

There are some things God will not permit us to know— that is, this side of going to heaven. In the meantime we try to figure Him out: Why does He have mercy on some and not others? What is the difference between what He allows and what He causes? Why did God create humankind knowing we would all suffer? Why does He allow evil? Why doesn't He stop it since He can?

We all want answers to these questions. The nearest you get to answering such questions is, that we might have faith. When Jesus learned that His friend Lazarus was critically ill, He could have made it to Bethany to heal him and keep him from dying. But no. He let Lazarus die. He then told the twelve that He did not heal Lazarus for their sakes in order that they might believe (John 11:15). Jesus intentionally let Lazarus die rather than heal him. It makes no sense at first. We likewise want to understand how the burning bush was not consumed. But God says *stop*. Take off your shoes. You are on holy ground.

God wants us to serve Him without getting all our questions answered.

These things said, we required to come to terms with the way we are wired, the way God made us. I have personally found it to be one of the most painful processes I have ever put myself through. Allow me to explain.

I have been a driven man all my life. My father pushed me to excel. My first job was selling *Grit* newspapers to my neighbors when I was ten. When I was twelve, I delivered the *Cincinnati Enquirer*—requiring me to get up at five o'clock every morning, then I had to be at school by 8:00 a.m. Years later I did the same with the *Ashland Daily Independent*, our local evening newspaper, which I delivered to 110 neighbors each afternoon when I got home from school. In addition to this, my father wanted me to make As in all subjects. He meant well, but I think he may have driven me a bit too hard. Partly as a result of this I became very ambitious. Being ambitious in my case has often led me to try to prove myself but also to think of myself more highly than I ought to think.

This is why I have found it painful to come to terms with the way God has made me. In a word, I am no Billy Graham. I am no Dr. Martyn Lloyd-Jones. I am no Jonathan Edwards. I am no Charles Haddon Spurgeon. But I wanted to be.

I did not have these sobering thoughts until I became the minister of Westminster Chapel at the age of forty-one. I never dreamed I would be there, but before I knew it, there I was, following G. Campbell Morgan (my father's favorite, 1863–1945), John Henry Jowett (a master pulpiteer, 1863–1923), and Dr. Martyn Lloyd-Jones (my chief mentor). The truth is, I never felt it was my pulpit—even after twenty-five years there. It was "the doctor's pulpit," meaning Dr. Martyn Lloyd-Jones. (He was always called "the doctor" by those who knew him.) At the same time, I felt it a duty at least to try to become a worthy successor to these giants.

It made things worse when I happened to preach a fairly

decent sermon, and well-meaning people would say of me, "A worthy successor to the doctor." Not true, of course. But I felt a need to try nonetheless. It was silly of me to have these thoughts in those days, but that's the truth— I foolishly tried. Oh, how I wish I could turn back the clock, then start over with the aim of coming to terms with the way God made me. I am not saying I would have had greater success, but I am sure I would have preached better. It is torture to keep trying to reach an unrealistic standard you set for yourself.

This shows God's kindness to us when He says we should not think of ourselves more highly than we should but to think soberly in accordance with the measure of faith He has given us (Rom. 12:3). Whereas it is deeply humbling, it lifts the pressure to achieve an unrealistic goal. One is set free. "Where the Spirit of the Lord is, there is freedom" (2 Cor. 3:17). The sooner we come to terms with the measure of faith—that is, the limit—God has given us, the sooner we will be at peace with ourselves.

In a word, it may be painful to come to terms with the limits of your gifting, but it's blissfully painless once you do accept the sovereign will of God for you and likewise the limits of your faith.

The Greek word translated "measure" in Romans 12:3 is *metron*. John 3:34 uses the same word, but there the NIV translates it as "limit," when John is referring to Jesus: "For the one whom God has sent speaks the words of God, for God gives the Spirit without limit." Jesus, therefore, had the Holy Spirit without measure—meaning no limit, or unlimited. You and I have faith in measure; there is a limit to our faith. Jesus had *all* of the Holy Spirit—*all there is of God*. This better explains why Paul is using the same Greek word—*metron*, translated "measure" but equally meaning limit. Our faith is sovereignly given in measure, meaning there is a limit to how much faith we have. God decides. Jesus didn't receive the Spirit in measure or limit; Jesus had all of God there is and likewise had perfect faith.

## THREE KINDS OF FAITH

There are at least three ways the word *faith*—in Greek, *pistis*—is used in the Bible.

1. *Saving faith*. That is transferring one's trust in good works to the finished work of Jesus Christ on the cross. This is the same as justifying faith, as in Romans 3:22, 27; 4:5; and 5:1. Jesus, of course, did not have this kind of faith; He did not need to be saved! But you and I need it; it is what ensures us of heaven when we die.

2. *Persistent faith*. "As you received Christ Jesus the Lord, so walk in him" (Col. 2:6). Persistent faith follows saving faith; it is what leads to our inheritance. Getting more of God is one way of describing our inheritance. We are all called to come into our inheritance—some do; some don't. Hebrews 11 describes those stalwarts who had persistent faith.

3. *The gift of faith.* This is the faith referred to
in Romans 12:3: "Think with sober judg-
ment, each according to the measure of
faith that God has assigned." It is not saving
faith, it is not persistent faith, but rather
it is faith given with reference to special
circumstances, as in your calling. You have
a limit of faith for this. This is the faith
referred to in the list of gifts of the Spirit in
1 Corinthians 12:9.

Here is what we need to know about this gift of faith.
It is what *God* gives. All gifts of the Spirit are sovereignly
bestowed; the Spirit gives them "as he wills" (1 Cor. 12:11).
"God arranged the members in the body [of Christ], each
one of them, as he chose" (1 Cor. 12:18).

This is crucial for us to grasp. It is the heart of the
matter. God is sovereign. We may rightly request of the
Lord, "Increase our faith" (Luke 17:5), and we should certainly "earnestly desire the higher gifts" (1 Cor. 12:31). But
the God who said to Moses, "I will have mercy on whom
I will have mercy, and I will have compassion on whom I
will have compassion" (Exod. 33:19, NIV) is the same God
who bestows faith in measure. God can give faith or withhold it and be just either way.

Not only that, but God determines the measure of our
success. If we are successful in what we do, He gets *all* the
glory. If we come short of our wishes for greater success,
the buck stops with Him.

This comforts me and sobers me. Paul said that it should

sober us. That is why he says for us "to think soberly" (Rom. 12:3, KJV). This means, "Don't live in a dream world about how successful you are going to be."

## ACCEPTING OUR NATURAL GIFTS

A well-known Christian leader in Britain once said, "If God had asked me what I would like to be, I would have said, 'A Jew,' because of their rich heritage. But He didn't." What would you like to be if you had a choice? In which century might you have chosen to be born? In which country? Which set of parents would you like? Do you wish you had been born a royal? Or aristocratic? A genius?

Not to worry. God has taken such out of our hands.

> The God who made the world and everything in it, being Lord of heaven and earth, does not live in temples made by man, nor is he served by human hands, as though he needed anything, since he himself gives to all mankind life and breath and everything. And he made from one man every nation of mankind to live on all the face of the earth, having determined allotted periods and the boundaries of their dwelling place, that they should seek God, and perhaps feel their way toward him and find him. Yet he is actually not far from each one of us.
>
> —ACTS 17:24–27

Like it or not, God chose our parents, the place and time of our births, and our natural abilities. Some theologians call it "common grace," God's goodness to all men and women. God's "special grace," said John Calvin

(1509–1564).[1] At the natural level we were given bodies, minds, likes and dislikes, propensities, talents, strengths, and weaknesses. It is not called "common" because it is ordinary but because God has given it commonly to all people. His sovereignty lies behind all these things. This means your talent, your IQ, the color of your hair and skin, your height, your physical features (whether you are plain or good looking), and your voice all come from the way God made you.

The issue is, Will you accept this? It does not mean you do not sometimes wish you were brighter, taller, or better looking. We are all shaped by our parents and, of course, environment. That bully on the playground, that horrible teacher, those who were jealous of you, or the fact that you were not brilliant in sports is integral to the way you are today.

You were known from the foundation of the world (Eph. 1:4). God knew you as if there were no one else on the planet, or as Saint Augustine put it, you are loved as though there were no one else to love.[2] Jesus said that the very hairs on our heads are numbered (Luke 12:7). That is how perfectly God knows each of us.

God wants two things for you and me: (1) to accept the way He made us and (2) to accept the limits of our faith. Accepting the limits of our faith is traceable to God's sovereign choice of our role in His kingdom. God made some people apostles, some prophets, some evangelists, some pastors, and some teachers (Eph. 4:11). He has chosen some to have specific gifts of the Holy Spirit (1 Cor. 12:8–10), some to be administrators, and some to have the gift to help others (v. 28). He has chosen some to have high-profile gifts—such as being the head or the eye of the body—and some to have low-profile gifts—such as being the kidneys or pancreas (vv. 14–24). All parts of the body are necessary to function; all gifts and profiles in the body of Christ are necessary for the church to function.

The question is, Will you accept the role God has *already* meted out for you? He made this decision when He created you and called you by His grace. In other words, God has already decided what He wants for you.

I'm sorry if this disappoints you or annoys you. But it is precisely why God said for each of us to think with sober judgment. God has given you and me a measure or limit of faith according to His creation and calling. It is why Paul said,

> Having gifts that differ according to the grace given to us, let us use them: if prophecy, in proportion to our faith; if service, in our serving; the one who teaches, in his teaching; the one who exhorts, in his exhortation; the one who contributes, in generosity; the one who leads, with zeal; the one who does acts of mercy, with cheerfulness.
>
> —ROMANS 12:6–8

## JEALOUSY

Nobody talks about the sin of jealousy. It comes into the picture when some of us have an ambition that exceeds our ability or surpasses what God already decided. Some promote themselves to the level of their incompetence.

They want leadership when they are not born leaders. They want to preach when in fact listening to them is deadly dull. They want to be in the spotlight when God made them "small intestines" in the body.

When Jesus told Peter how he would die, Peter could only think about John. Here is the background, when Jesus said to Peter:

> "I tell you the truth, when you were young...you dressed yourself and went wherever you wanted to go. But when you are old, you will stretch out your hands, and others will dress you and take you where you don't want to go." Jesus said this to let him know by what kind of death he would glorify God. Then Jesus told him, "Follow me!"
>
> Peter turned around and saw behind them the disciple Jesus loved....Peter asked Jesus, "What about him, Lord?"
>
> Jesus replied, "If I want him to remain alive until I return, what is that to you? As for you, follow me."
> —JOHN 21:18–22, NLT

Instead of accepting what Jesus had already decided about how Peter should die, Peter wanted to know how John would die! Jesus in effect said, "None of your business. You follow Me."

I urge you to let this passage grip you. What Jesus ordered for Peter is the same thing God orders for each of us in His kingdom. He has given us a measure of faith. He has given us a calling in His kingdom. He has given us a gift in His service. He has given us a certain responsibility in the body of Christ. For some, it will be high profile; for others, low profile—like being an organ in the body that is not visible the way the head, eye, ear, and hand are visible.

We may not like the way God has made us. We may not like where we were born. We may feel cheated by the parents He gave us. We may be disappointed with the responsibility we have in His kingdom. The question is, Will we reflect soberly and come to terms with where God has put us in His body?

As I said previously, our anointing is connected to our extent of influence. That does not mean that the greatest preacher will reach the most people or that the dullest preacher will reach the least people. Although I regard Billy Graham as a great preacher, I equally accept that there are communicators with greater preaching skills who don't reach as many people as he did. Indeed, I know some very good evangelists who reach a minute portion of the population compared with the 220 million people to whom Billy preached. I also know some who aspire to be "the next Billy Graham," "the Billy Graham of Italy," or "the Billy Graham of Brazil." But they are not Billy Graham and don't even come close to having his influence.

This is why we must accept two further things: (1) the measure, or limit, of our anointing and (2) the measure, or limit, of our influence. The reason some can "out-preach" Billy Graham but do not have his influence is simple: it is because of the sovereign purpose of God. They may try to open doors or knock them down to be more famous or widely used, but they are honestly kidding themselves.

You may say, "This chapter does not apply to me because I am not a preacher, and I am not ever going to be center stage in God's kingdom." I reply, "For by the grace given me I say to *every one of you*: Do not think of yourself more highly than you ought" (Rom. 12:3, NIV, emphasis added). Paul is addressing every single Christian! There are those who prophesy, and there are those whose ministry is encouragement. We must all come to terms with our "motivational gifts," as some would call them.

As for prophesying, Paul says we must prophesy "in proportion" to our faith (Rom. 12:6). This means we stay *within the limits* of what God has shown us. Some would say that prophesying in Romans 12:6 refers to preaching. I doubt this. I think Paul is addressing those with prophetic gifts, those who get a word from God and want to share it. Paul is saying that such people should never go beyond what they are given—no matter how tempted they might be to embellish the word.

The same is true with all gifts referred to in Romans 12: prophesying, serving, teaching, encouraging, giving, leading, and showing mercy. In a word, we should *discover our niche* in the body of Christ—and stay put. Nobody can do everything. Even if someone has more than one of these motivational gifts—one may be a leader and also a teacher; one may have the gift of helping others and also be prophetic. But one must think *soberly* and not promote oneself to a level to which one has not been called of God.

It might be painful to be a better preacher than Billy Graham and only reach dozens rather than thousands. Yes. And this is why we should live "in accordance" with the measure of faith—or measure of success—God has given us. Your brain might be more magnificent than Jonathan Edwards', who was probably the greatest theologian in American history, but God may choose to hide you for His glory.

"That does not make sense to me," you may say. That was my friend Paul Hilton's problem. He could not accept the possibility that he could be a genius and not be used of God. Who knows what God might have done with him had he not rebelled. I, therefore, urge you, if you are somewhat like that, get your joy from knowing that at the judgment seat of Christ you will be glad you accepted God's role and will for you.

What if you are the CEO of a corporation but only an usher or steward in church? What if you are the president of a company but are not given a high-profile position in your church? What if you are a university graduate, a lawyer, an accountant, a physician, or a professor but have a minimal profile in God's work? Can you live with this? What if you are in the habit of telling people what to do all week but when you come to church, you must listen to God's servant reveal the Word of God to you?

Accepting the limits of our faith is humbling. It is humbling to accept a high-profile gift too. The issue is, What honors God in your situation?

> Ye saints, who toil below, adore your heav'nly King,
> And onward as ye go some joyful anthem sing;
> Take what he gives and praise him still
> Through good and ill, who ever lives.[3]

—RICHARD BAXTER (1615–1691)

Yes. Take what He gives. Accept it. Don't grumble. Don't complain. Don't be jealous of the one who has a gift or position you might have wanted.

If you and I want more of God, this is a way of showing it. A huge way. It won't do for us to keep saying, "I love you, Lord," or "All I want is You," or even "I'm desperate for You." We show how much we want more of God by accepting His will. This proves we want more of Him because this way we dignify His will.

# Chapter 5

# THE GLORY

*For they loved the glory that comes from man
more than the glory that comes from God.*
—JOHN 12:43

KEEP THE GLORY down."[1] Those were the oft repeated words of Dr. Phineas Bresee (1838–1915), founder of my old denomination, the Church of the Nazarene. Before he died, he went from church to church with this message. Why? It was because the early Nazarenes were by and large short on great intellects, people with money, and those who were well connected. But they had one thing—the "glory," as he called it. He feared they would lose this.

I know what he meant by that. Although I was a third-generation Nazarene, my old church in Ashland, Kentucky, still had a touch of what Bresee called the "glory." It was the presence of God that manifested in people shouting, running, crying, and jumping. I grew up seeing this. The neighbors called us "Noisyrenes." I vividly recall people walking the aisles—sometimes running and shouting, "Glory, glory, glory." Akin to this are the words in Psalm 29:9: "And in his temple all cry, 'Glory!'" It was spontaneous. No doubt there was a lot of flesh that moved in. It always does. But it was still what almost certainly gave the Church of the Nazarene—founded in 1908—its rapid growth. Bresee knew that if they ever lost this, they were finished.

When I first came to England, in 1973, and began to get better acquainted with Dr. and Mrs. Martyn Lloyd-Jones, my Nazarene background is what largely endeared me to them. He had just read a biography of Dr. Bresee and was convinced there was something genuine about the early Nazarenes. "Don't forget your Nazarene background," he said to me again and again. "That is what has saved you." He felt it saved me from being hard and cold like so many reformed people who, he feared, had become "perfectly orthodox, perfectly useless." On the night Westminster Chapel voted to call me its minister, he phoned me with this advice: "Preach like a Nazarene."

## USES OF THE WORD GLORY

The word *glory* embraces both the tangible and the intangible. The tangible means something that can be visible and experienced; it became known as the Shekinah, a word that appeared first in rabbinic literature. The intangible refers largely to the *source* of one's approval, praise, and honor. In a word, do you want the praise that comes from men or the praise that comes from God?

We should examine two words in the ancient languages that translate "glory."

## 1. Kabod

In the Old Testament it is *kabod*. It is a word that means heaviness—as in weight or stature. It is like when people throw their weight around. That is partly the idea of *kabod*. However, this can be applied to times when the Holy Spirit comes down in power—the result being a holy heaviness in the atmosphere.

Mrs. Martyn Lloyd-Jones, who personally experienced the Welsh Revival (1904–1905), used to talk to me about it. Her father put her on a train at Paddington Station, London, after taking her out of school so she could witness the Welsh Revival. "She can always go to school," her father said, "but she may never see revival again." She spoke of an atmosphere in which she would at times slightly gasp for breath, even though she was a child of six at the time of the revival. Others, experiencing the phenomenon of the Toronto Blessing, have testified to a weight on them so that they could not move. A number of people have recounted to me very similar experiences. Having fallen to the floor under the power of the Spirit, they said, "I told this person to get off my back so I could get up, but there was no one there."

## 2. Doxa

The Greek word *doxa* translates "glory." It is the word from which *doxology* comes. It means praise or honor. It comes from a root word that means opinion. By this rendering the glory of God is His opinion or will. This fits with Paul's words: "In him we have obtained an inheritance, having been predestined according to the purpose of him who works all things according to the counsel of his will, so that we who were the first to hope in Christ might be to the praise of his *glory*" (Eph. 1:11–12, emphasis added). Taking our cue from *doxa*, the glory of God is the dignity of His will. Those who choose the glory or praise from people forfeit the honor or praise that would have come from God—which is precisely what the Pharisees of Jesus' day did. They loved the praise that came from people more than the praise that comes from God (John 5:44; 12:43). The consequence of this was that they missed their Messiah.

*Kabod* and *doxa* combined means the way God *chooses* to manifest Himself. He is sovereign; we cannot twist His arm to make Him do what we may wish for.

## THE WORD MADE FLESH

God manifested Himself in the flesh—Jesus Christ of Nazareth. He is *kabod* and *doxa* combined. "The Word became flesh and dwelt among us, and we have seen his glory," said John, "glory as of the only Son from the Father, full of grace and truth" (John 1:14).

God has manifested His glory in countless ways ever since. While Jesus was on this earth, the glory of God was shone through teaching, preaching, healing, and miracles. The first miracle was changing the water into wine. "He revealed His *glory*, and His disciples believed in Him" (John 2:11, MEV, emphasis added). When Jesus raised Lazarus from the dead, it was a manifestation of the glory of God (John 11:4, 40).

## OUR PRAYER COVENANT

I introduced a Prayer Covenant at Westminster Chapel in 1994. Some three hundred people signed up to pray daily for, among other things, "the manifestation of God's glory in our midst along with an ever-increasing openness in us to the way He chooses to manifest that glory." I knew that God could show up in surprising and uncomfortable ways. I also knew that most of the British members of Westminster Chapel were probably not prepared for some of the ways God has manifested His glory in church history. As I mentioned in a previous chapter, after Jonathan Edwards preached his sermon "Sinners in the Hands of an Angry God" (1741), people held on to church pews and tree trunks to keep from sliding into hell.

At the Cane Ridge revival (1801) in Bourbon County, Kentucky, hundreds fell to the ground—and lay there for hours—under the power of the Holy Spirit. I wanted our people to be open to the way God may choose! What I hoped for was a manifestation of the *kabod*. In the end the way God chose to manifest His glory was largely by withholding the *kabod* from us. We accepted the dignity of His will, *doxa*—namely, largely to *pass us by* and bless churches such as Holy Trinity Brompton with the *kabod* instead. After all, God is sovereign. To dignify His will—whatever it is—is to bring Him the highest honor.

## OTHER USES OF THE WORD GLORY

### The total of all His attributes

The glory of God is the nearest you get to the "essence" of His being. Consider the various attributes of God: omniscience (He knows all), omnipresence (He is everywhere), omnipotence (He is all powerful; He can do anything), sovereignty (He has mercy on whom He will have mercy on), justice (He is fair and is determined to punish evil), mercy (He does not want to punish us), holiness (He will not tolerate sin), love (He is tender toward all His creation), and wrath (He feels anger toward sin). The total of all these attributes is glory. The glory of God is the sum of all His attributes. It is the one word that embraces all these attributes simultaneously. Hence Stephen referred to Him as the "God of glory" (Acts 7:2).

### The Shekinah

The rabbis used this word to describe what is supernatural—that is, what is beyond or above the natural. It is the transliteration of a Hebrew word that means dwelling or settling of the divine presence of God. It is a word used to describe what is truly miraculous, that which defies a natural explanation. For example:

> Then the cloud covered the tent of meeting, and the glory of the LORD filled the tabernacle. And Moses was not able to enter the tent of meeting because the cloud settled on it, and the glory of the LORD filled

the tabernacle. Throughout all their journeys, when-
ever the cloud was taken up from over the tabernacle, the people of Israel would set out. But if the
cloud was not taken up, then they did not set out
till the day that it was taken up. For the cloud of
the LORD was on the tabernacle by day, and fire was
in it by night, in the sight of all the house of Israel
throughout all their journeys.

—EXODUS 40:34–38

## The Shekinah on Good Friday

From noon until 3:00 p.m. on Good Friday, "there was
darkness over all the land" (Matt. 27:45). This was *not* an
eclipse of the sun, as some have conjectured. It was the
Shekinah—the cloud that came down as a divine witness
to Jesus' shed blood. When God introduced the Day of
Atonement to Moses, He promised to "appear in the cloud
over the mercy seat" (Lev. 16:2). That cloud was a dark
cloud. When the cloud filled the temple upon the arrival
of the ark of the covenant, the priests could not perform
their service: "the glory of the LORD filled the house of
God" (2 Chron. 5:14). Then Solomon said, "The LORD has
said that he would dwell in thick darkness" (2 Chron. 6:1).
The darkness on Good Friday was precisely this—a seal of
God upon the atonement of Jesus' death on the cross.

## The Shekinah in more recent times

I once heard Pastor Jack Hayford, possibly the most
respected Charismatic leader in America, tell of an event
that took place in his church years ago on a Saturday. He
looked inside the auditorium and saw a haze. "It's what
you think it is," the Lord said to him. This happened

when his church was young, with an attendance of perhaps three hundred. After that day his church began to grow and grow until it reached thousands. Jack traces this growth to that Saturday when he saw the haze.

In April 1956 at my old church in Ashland, Kentucky, a lay member—Ed Lynn—interrupted the service. He began walking up and down the front and center aisle and shouting that "Ichabod" (meaning the glory has departed) was written over the church. A haze came over the auditorium, and controversy erupted. Many who were present felt that Ed was in the flesh and out of order. Others saw it as a wonderful manifestation of God's presence. I will add two things here: (1) that service was to change my life forever, and (2) my old church afterward gradually began to diminish in numbers and support. What was once one of the most strategic and influential churches in the denomination became small and insignificant. I interpret the haze to be a seal of God on the service, to mean that Ed's word that the glory has departed was prophetic.

Do you want more of God? If so, you must *love* the glory of God, which means you must appreciate the way He chooses to show up—however uncomfortable it makes you feel—but also accept His will—no matter how disappointed you may be. Jonathan Edwards taught that the one thing Satan *cannot* do is give one a love for God's glory. If you love the way God shows up, it is a good sign that you want more of God; if you love what God chooses to do, it is a good sign that you want more of God.

## EMPTY GLORY

If you love the praise of people more than the glory that comes from God, you are in a vast company. But such recognition is an empty glory. It became the downfall of the Pharisees: they lived for the praise of one another. All they did was "to be seen by others" (Matt. 23:5), whether it was their giving to the poor (Matt. 6:1–4), their praying (vv. 5–8), or their fasting (vv. 16–18). Having people admire their pious acts meant the world to them. But, said Jesus, such admiration was their ultimate and only reward. There would be no more reward for them; the praise of people *was it*. It did not cross their minds to pursue the honor that comes from God only (John 5:44). That was not on their radar screen. Such thinking was utterly alien to them. They got glory for sure, but it was an empty glory— meaningless, vain, and worthless.

Ironically, craving the praise of man is rooted in the fear of man. The people were afraid to say good things about Jesus lest they be put out of the synagogue. "Nevertheless, many even of the authorities believed in him, but for fear of the Pharisees they did not confess it, so that they would not be put out of the synagogue; for they loved the glory that comes from man more than the glory that comes from God" (John 12:42–43). The fear of man is a snare (Prov. 29:25).

Many people miss what God is doing in our day for the same reason. There were those who were afraid to affirm the Welsh Revival lest they lose friends. There are those who stayed away from the Toronto Blessing because they

feared rejection. I know of famous missionaries who were
rejected by the church that supported them because they
went to Toronto and got prayed for. They went to Toronto
because they wanted more of God—that is all they wanted!
They chose the praise of God rather than the affirmation
of their church. They lost their church's support but have
founded thousands of churches in Mozambique, Africa.

Two figures in the Bible built monuments to themselves.
The first was King Saul. At Carmel he "set up a monument
for himself" (1 Sam. 15:12). Imagine how pitiful. He made
a choice—to have a monument built for his own honor
rather than wait for the honor that might have come
from God. His life ended in unspeakable tragedy—suicide
(1 Sam. 31:4).

The other person was Absalom, a son of David. "Now
Absalom in his lifetime had taken and set up for himself
the pillar that is in the King's Valley, for he said, 'I have
no son to keep my name in remembrance.' He called the
pillar after his own name, and it is called Absalom's monument to this day" (2 Sam. 18:18). He was the man who
turned against his father, King David, and stole the hearts
of the people. It led to David abandoning his throne in
Jerusalem for a while. God later restored David to the
throne while removing Absalom, whose life also ended
tragically (2 Sam. 18:15).

It is striking that both Saul and Absalom regarded
David as their common enemy. Both Saul and Absalom
wanted to leave a mark on their generation. They cared
about how people would remember them. By contrast,
David prayed: "Deliver my soul...from men by your hand,

O LORD, from men of the world whose portion is *in this life*" (Ps. 17:13–14, emphasis added).

This life is not all there is. There is more. We will one day stand before the judgment seat of Christ (2 Cor. 5:10). What is decided then and there will eclipse what we deemed important in the here and now. Our lives on earth will determine the ultimate verdict—God's opinion of how we lived.

Empty glory. That is what the devil wants to give you. That is what one gets who seeks his or her own glory. Saul did it. Absalom did it. The Pharisees did it. Empty glory goes to those who want the praise of people more than the praise of God. When you want more of God than any other thing in this world, you must beware the praise of people lest you miss the praise that God wants to give you.

## MOSES' REQUESTS

Moses made two requests to God that are worth examining here. The first was this: "Now therefore, if I have found favor in your sight, please show me now your ways, that I may know you in order to find favor in your sight" (Exod. 33:13). Do you remember when I shared about reading this verse on a plane from New York to Miami—as if for the first time? It shook me rigid from head to toe. I felt so convicted. It was as though all my requests for more anointing appeared vain. What was my motive for more anointing? I could see how selfish it was. But by contrast, Moses' request was for more of God: "show me now your ways, that *I may know you.*" Which now would I choose—more anointing or to know God's ways? Paul's supreme desire: "I want to know Christ" (Phil. 3:10, NIV).

I fear my desire for a greater anointing was merely wanting more *from* God; it would help me teach better and preach better. But what Moses wanted was more *of* God—to know Him.

How many of us want to know God for His own sake—just to know Him, to know *what He is like*? Forget what God might do for us for the moment; what is He like? Do I want to know what God is like? To know Him as He is in Himself? To know His ways? What if He never used me again—would I still want to know Him and to know His ways? Do I serve God only for what He can do for me? Do I care what He is like?

These questions stagger me. They reveal my motives. It is embarrassing. That said, part of the fallout of seeing the glory is seeing our sin. Isaiah saw the glory of the Lord and then cried, "Woe is me! For I am lost; for I am a man of unclean lips" (Isa. 6:5).

The other request Moses made was "Please show me your glory" (Exod. 33:18). His desire may have been for the *kabod*—to see the tangible glory of God. Who wouldn't want to see this? But what he got was a bare touch of the *kabod* and a massive revelation of *doxa*—God's opinion:

> And he said, "I will make all my goodness pass before you and will proclaim before you my name 'The Lord.' And I will be gracious to whom I will be gracious, and will show mercy on whom I will show

mercy. But," he said, "you cannot see my face, for man shall not see me and live."

—Exodus 33:19–20

This moment taught Moses the sovereignty of God. He had seen earlier that God is a jealous God, which was initially revealed in the Ten Commandments (Exod. 20:5). But at the Tent of Meeting, Moses was told that God would have mercy on whom He would have mercy and be gracious to whom He would be gracious. Paul repeated this in Romans 9 when he unfolded more of the sovereignty of God (Rom. 9:15ff.). The sovereignty of God is His prerogative to do what He chooses to do with whomever He wants. It is part of the privilege of being God, if I may put it that way. We, therefore, must let God be God.

That is what Moses learned. However close Moses got to God, Moses could only receive what God decided to give.

And the Lord said, "Behold, there is a place by me where you shall stand on the rock, and while my glory passes by I will put you in a cleft of the rock, and I will cover you with my hand until I have passed by. Then I will take away my hand, and you shall see my back, but my face shall not be seen."

—Exodus 33:21–23

Moses could never demand something of God. He would only ask. He would always be on the begging end. Remember, we must approach God as the leper approached Jesus in Matthew 8:2. As John the Baptist put it, "A person cannot receive even one thing unless it is given him from heaven" (John 3:27).

Moses was only allowed to see God's back—a mere reflection of the *kabod*. But in the face of Jesus Christ we see the full glory of God. God has given us the "light of the knowledge of the glory of God in the face of Jesus Christ" (2 Cor. 4:6).

The sovereignty of God, the jealousy of God, and the glory of God are intertwined. Moses learned this. He first asked to know God's ways. He then asked to see God's glory. And the answer came: "I will have mercy on whom I will have mercy."

How does that make you feel? Do you want a God like that? Caution: if you don't love a God like that, it may well suggest you don't want more *of* Him. Jonathan Edwards said that the devil cannot give you a love for the glory of God; it is what God alone can impart. The flesh won't give you a love for God's glory; the flesh profits "nothing" (John 6:63, NIV). But if you and I have a genuine love for the glory of God, it shows that God is sovereignly at work in us. It means we have an unfeigned relationship with God, one that is not counterfeit. The flesh cannot give you a love for the glory of God or the God of glory. But if you love the God of glory—the God who is jealous and sovereign—you may be fully assured: you show you are a person who wants more of God.

## AN AUDIENCE OF ONE

Have you ever wondered how it was that the Jews missed their Messiah? They had prayed for generations, "Oh that you would rend the heavens and come down" (Isa. 64:1). There was not a Pharisee or Sadducee who thought that Messiah would come and he would miss him. These people thought it was impossible for Messiah to appear and not be recognized by them. They were like a minister in London who wrote to me, "If revival comes to London, I'll know it." Really?

The Jews missed their promised Messiah because, as John put it, "They loved the glory that comes from man more than the glory that comes from God" (John 12:43). This is why Jesus posed this question to them: "How can you believe, when you receive glory from one another and do not seek the glory that comes from the only God?" (John 5:44). The answer: you can't. How can you believe when you choose the praise of men rather than the praise of God? You can't.

Jesus, therefore, showed an inseparable connection between the ability to believe and one's pursuit of the praise of God. It goes to show that a desire to get more of God has a fringe benefit: an increase of your faith. Not only that; you are not likely to miss what God is doing today. Jonathan Edwards taught us that the task of every generation is to discover in which direction the sovereign Redeemer is moving, then move in that direction. But how are you going to know in which direction the sovereign Redeemer is moving? Answer: it will become apparent when you make an effort to obtain His approval versus the praise that comes from people.

The Pharisees wanted an audience of many. The more, the better if they might demonstrate their piety. They lived not only to please people; they craved the admiration of everybody. It became their motive to be "godly," but they, like some of the English Puritans, loved godliness more than God.

An audience of One—only God—did not appeal to them. But Jesus wanted His followers to be different. Look at His instructions in Matthew 6:

- When it comes to giving, we should do it in secret—not before men—so that our Father, "who sees in secret," will reward us (v. 4).

- When it comes to praying, we are likewise instructed to go into a room and close the door so that our Father, "who sees in secret," will reward us (v. 6).

- When we fast, we are not to let it show but fast before an audience of One, "who sees in secret," and He will reward us (v. 18).

Does Jesus' teaching grip you? I hope so. It means you want more and more of God. It means you are making an effort to eschew the praise of people in order to have the praise of a jealous God.

Malachi said, "Then those who feared the LORD spoke with one another. The LORD paid attention and heard them." Though they talked with one another, they were conscious of an audience of One. "A book of remembrance was written before him of those who feared the LORD and esteemed his name" (Mal. 3:16). Jesus said, "I tell you, on the day of judgment people will give account for every careless word they speak" (Matt. 12:36). When we talk with one another, we should be conscious of God more than one another. He is listening. He is watching. As the old spiritual put it:

> He sees all you do, He hears all you say;
> My Lord is writing all the time, time, time;
> He sees all you do, He hears all you say;
> My Lord is writing all the time.[2]
>
> —Anonymous

This is scary! But there is hope if we are convicted of our carelessness and lack of seeking the honor that comes from God only.

This teaching should affect those of us who are teachers or preachers. This principle governed the apostle Paul. He said that when he preached, he spoke before God—an audience of One. "We preach the word of God with sincerity and with Christ's authority, knowing that God is watching us" (2 Cor. 2:17, NLT).

I'm afraid I have failed miserably in this area. I remember preaching in Bournemouth, England, twenty-five years ago. It was to the Easter People (as they were called then), to perhaps two thousand people. I wanted to do well and did my best. Normally someone will come up to the speaker immediately and say, "Thank you for your word," or something like that. But nobody said a word. I am ashamed to admit that I hung around for several minutes, hoping that *someone* would give me an encouraging word. My hanging around was a dead giveaway that I was not preaching to an audience of One but of two thousand.

Feeling I did not do well, I got in my car and struggled

to enjoy the two-hour journey back to London. I asked the Lord, "What do You think of my sermon tonight?" Not that He always answers a request like that, but I can tell you I got *nothing* from the Lord. I got over it in a day or two and then forgot about it until a year ago when I was preaching in Wembley, London.

A lady came up to me and said, "You won't remember this, but twenty-five years ago you preached to the Easter People in Bournemouth."

I replied, "Oh yes, I do; I remember that service well."

"Really?" she asked. "I was converted that night."

I was amazed. It was the first clue that I had not done too bad. It also shows that God overrules those of us who forget the audience of One and hope to please people.

I've quoted John 5:44 in this book and in most of the books I have written. Over the years I have sought to be governed by this verse. I have failed many, many times. Even in writing this book, I find myself bordering on wanting to do an excellent job in writing but aiming (please, God) to get the praise from Him only.

It is a lofty goal—to aspire to the praise of God and not man's approval. It is easy to be a Pharisee. One does not have to go to university to learn how to be a Pharisee. It is proof of what theologians call original sin. It is in all of us.

What, then, is the praise that comes from the only God? I think two things. First, God sometimes graciously gives us an inner testimony of the Spirit. It is a sweet feeling that you genuinely endeavored to please Him alone—and He lets you know it. It's so good. Second, it will all come out at the judgment seat of Christ. It is when Jesus will look at us and (hopefully) say, "Well done."

I want that more than anything.

# Chapter 6

# THE SUPERSTRUCTURE

*For no one can lay a foundation other than that which*
*is laid, which is Jesus Christ. Now if anyone builds on*
*the foundation with gold, silver, precious stones, wood,*
*hay, straw—each one's work will become manifest, for*
*the Day will disclose it, because it will be revealed*
*by fire, and the fire will test what sort of work each*
*one has done. If the work that anyone has built on*
*the foundation survives, he will receive a reward. If*
*anyone's work is burned up, he will suffer loss, though*
*he himself will be saved, but only as through fire.*
—1 CORINTHIANS 3:11–15

I MENTIONED THE CANE Ridge Revival (1801) in the previous chapter. I talk about it a lot wherever I go. I referred to it in several of my books, including *Stand Up and Be Counted*, which has a brief foreword written by Billy Graham. In *A Prophet With Honor: The Billy*

*Graham Story* the author, William Martin, mentions the Cane Ridge Revival. He rightly calls it America's "second Great Awakening."[1] In the British Museum I researched the revival years ago and followed up by reading about it as much as I could since living in Hendersonville, Tennessee. The spark that ignited the revival came in a place near the Red River at the Kentucky/Tennessee border in 1800—just an hour away from where we now live in Hendersonville. The Holy Spirit fell in great power at a communion service in a Presbyterian church, and people agreed to meet the following year in Cane Ridge, Kentucky. It was the beginning of the camp meetings when thousands came in their covered wagons to Bourbon County, Kentucky, to an area known as Cane Ridge for fellowship and Bible study.

I remember some accounts mention that on Sunday morning, August 9, 1801, a Methodist lay preacher stood on the top of a fallen tree and began preaching on 2 Corinthians 5:10:

> For we must all appear before the judgment seat of Christ; that every one may receive the things done in his body, according to that he hath done, whether it be good or bad.
>
> —2 CORINTHIANS 5:10, KJV

Approximately fifteen thousand people stood as they listened. Hundreds fell spontaneously to the ground. No one was praying for them. Nobody pushed them. They just fell. Panic set in, some fearing they were dead. But after a few hours these same people came up shouting with joy and assurance of their salvation. Others began falling as well.

Between Sunday and Wednesday, never fewer than five hundred people fell flat out on the ground.[2] One participant said, "The noise was like the roar of Niagara" because of the large number of people.[3] On the following Thursday most of the people headed for their homes and returned to their jobs.

The Cane Ridge Revival only lasted for five or six days. The New England Great Awakening lasted for fifteen years or more (approximately 1735 to 1750). We can trace the existence of a Bible Belt in America to these two awakenings.[4] Some historians believe the New England Great Awakening led directly to the Declaration of Independence on July 4, 1776.

The two awakenings had this in common: *the focus on what happens when we die.* What grips me about both revivals is the importance of life beyond the grave. So much preaching today is about the here and now; it often comes from an existential perspective, even if those who preach it could not define that term. We are in the "me" generation, and people flock to hear the "feel-good" type of teaching. It is my view that a great awakening is coming. When it comes, it will mean a restoration of the pure gospel, along with a robust teaching of heaven and hell. Please see my book *Whatever Happened to the Gospel?*

The focus of this chapter is on the judgment seat of Christ and how we might prepare for it. The degree to which you want more of God will be revealed and rewarded at the judgment seat of Christ.

I titled this chapter "The Superstructure" because there are two dimensions to be considered when it comes to wanting more of God: (1) wanting more of Him in the here and now and (2) what this will mean at the judgment seat of Christ. Paul prepares us for the judgment seat of Christ by a *metaphor*—showing two things: (1) the foundation of a building and (2) the superstructure on that foundation.

The foundation is Jesus Christ. Either you are on the foundation, or you are not. If you are on it, you are saved; you are "in Christ" and will go to heaven when you die (2 Cor. 5:17; see also v. 21; Eph. 4:1). If you are not on it, you are lost and will go to hell when you die. Furthermore, there is no possibility of building a superstructure if you are not on the foundation. Therefore, whether you are saved or lost is determined by whether you are *on* that foundation. Once on it, you are eternally saved. You cannot fall off that foundation. You can fall on it but not off it. As Charles Spurgeon (1834–1892) put it, you can be on a great ship and slip or fall on it, but you will not fall off it. I do not intend to defend this teaching here, but you might read my book *Once Saved, Always Saved* if it is a teaching you would love to understand further.

These things said, if you are on Christ, the foundation, there is a superstructure to be built if you want more of God and a reward at the judgment seat of Christ. The quality of the superstructure determines whether you will receive a reward at the judgment seat of Christ.

## MATERIALS THAT GO INTO THE SUPERSTRUCTURE

Paul has chosen the metaphor of gold, silver, precious stones, wood, hay, and straw to illustrate how rewards are

meted out at the judgment seat of Christ. On "the day"—
meaning the day of the judgment seat of Christ—*fire*
will declare the quality of our superstructure. To know
what Paul means by that, ask this question: Of those
ingredients—wood, hay, straw, gold, silver, and precious
stones—what can burn up? Wood? Yes. Hay? Yes. Straw?
Yes. Gold? No. Silver? No. Precious stones? No.

These ingredients refer to our works (our deeds and
actions). Good works will not save us (Eph. 2:8–9), but
they will determine our reward at the judgment seat of
Christ. Works, therefore, matter. They don't contribute to
being saved; the foundation guarantees that. But works
go into the superstructure. At the judgment seat of Christ,
God will reward your good works—represented in the
metaphor of gold, silver, and precious stones. Fire will not
destroy these. Bad works, however, are seen in the metaphor of wood, hay, and straw.

You may ask, "Can a truly saved person have bad works?"
Sadly yes. Do you ever lose your temper? Do you ever show
jealous feelings? Do you ever hold a grudge? Do you ever
say things that are out of order—like when a small spark
ignites a forest fire (Jas. 3:5)? I could go on and on.

Picture these six ingredients lumped together, and then
imagine pouring gasoline, or petrol, on them, striking a
match, and dropping it onto the pile. After a couple of
minutes, what would you find? Only the gold, silver, and
precious stones. The wood, hay, and straw would be burnt
up. On the day of judgment God will send the fire to determine the quality of our superstructure. Our bad works—
wood, hay, and straw—will be burnt up. If there are

good works—gold, silver, and precious stones—they will survive, *and*, says Paul, if what we have built survives, we will receive a reward (1 Cor. 3:14). But suppose one's superstructure is constructed entirely of wood, hay, and straw. Paul answers in verse 15: "If anyone's work is burned up, he will suffer loss [of reward], though he himself will be saved [because he is on the foundation], but only as through fire." (The King James Version says "by fire.") According to this, it is possible—at least in theory—for a saved person to have no good works to show at the judgment seat of Christ.

I would personally prefer to believe that the absence of good works of a truly saved man or woman is in theory only, but only God is the judge. "Therefore do not pronounce judgment before the time, before the Lord comes, who will bring to light the things now hidden in darkness and will disclose the purposes of the heart. Then each one will receive his commendation from God" (1 Cor. 4:5).

I often quote Martin Luther as saying he expected three surprises when he got to heaven: (1) those he was surprised to see; (2) those missing that he expected to see; and (3) that he would be there himself! If I may paraphrase Luther, I too expect three surprises at the judgment seat of Christ: (1) there will be those who receive a reward that will surprise me; (2) there will be those saved by fire that I thought would have a reward; and (3) that I, myself, will receive a reward at the judgment seat of Christ!

The question follows: What are good works? The answer: they are works done in obedience to the Word of God. To repeat, Paul's metaphors for such are gold, silver, and precious stones. What are bad works? The answer: works done by those who are disobedient to the Word of God. Paul's metaphors for such are wood, hay, and straw.

## Examples of Works Built With Gold, Silver, and Precious Stones

### Sound doctrine

We are responsible for what we believe. Yes, you will be rewarded at the judgment seat of Christ for upholding the *truth* of God. You should be wise enough to detect heresy—any teaching that deviates from Holy Scripture. We are indeed responsible for upholding the truth. If you are tossed to and fro by every wind of doctrine, this is not good. Not good at all. You are not responsible for being clever, intellectual, educated, or brilliant. It is what your *heart* longs for, seeking after the truth of God, that matters. It includes being unashamed of the infallibility of the Bible. The words of Jesus help us make this connection in John 7:17: "If anyone's will is to do God's will, he will know whether the teaching is from God or whether I am speaking on my own authority."

What is crucial: a love of the truth. If you have a love of the *truth*—wherever it leads and whatever the cost—you are going to be in good shape. No matter what teaching or teacher you must abandon, find the truth of the Bible and uphold it. The way to know you are not being misled is that you earnestly desire to do God's will. If you genuinely want to know God's will and persevere to know it, you may be sure you will not be led astray when it comes to teaching. The assumption here too is that you know your Bible. Do you?

86

Many years ago, when I was still at seminary in Louisville, Kentucky, I seriously considered going to Germany to obtain a doctorate. I met someone who insisted that I needed to go there if I wanted to think deeply and wrestle with the most profound ideas. I was set on it. In the providence of God a professor at my old seminary by the name of Dr. Wayne Ward (1921–2012) cautioned me. He told me something I did not realize and had never thought of— namely, that to get a German doctorate, you don't need to be seeking after truth but to come up with any idea that will be striking enough that they will award you a doctorate. They are not after the truth in the theology departments of German universities, said Dr. Ward, but any novel idea that has not been put forward before. It sobered me, but it also saved me from a horrendous decision.

It also gave me pause when thinking about the many, many German theologians of the last two centuries who have been so influential—always starting new trends but never ending up with solid truth. I would like to believe that there are exceptions. However, "It is not the truth they are after," said Dr. Ward, but "any innovative idea that might lead to becoming a professor." He added that the professors I would be studying under got their doctorates this same way. "You would not be studying with men who want the truth." This was merely Dr. Ward's opinion at the time, of course, and one would hope things are different now. But to this day I thank God for Dr. Ward and his warning.

If you want *truth*, says Jesus, seek to know and follow the Father's will, fully surrendering your personal, private life to Him. Truth is not apprehended by being intellectual, cerebral, or clever but by your obedience to Holy Scripture. That was Jesus' defense when being confronted by the Jews of His day. If Jews wanted to know whether His teaching was from God, He told them to seek and follow God's will.

The way you show you want more of God is by reading His Word regularly, consistently, and with the view of grasping the doctrinal truth of His Word. You don't need to be an articulate theologian, but you need to know what you believe—and why. Being able to recognize and resist what is not true is equal to learning how to recognize and resist the devil. Sound doctrine is essential to a strong superstructure, which will stand the test of fire at the judgment seat of Christ.

One more thing: I have come to the place that I now say, if you want to know what the Bible teaches, ask a liberal! Ask a liberal what the Bible says about hell, gay marriage, open theism, and universalism. Liberals know because that is precisely why they are liberal and no longer believe the Bible! But the situation has changed much in recent years. What we have today is a rising tide of people who want to call themselves evangelical and hold to biblical infallibility but who have convinced themselves of every teaching from universalism to annihilation, from gay marriage to open theism.

I say as lovingly and as firmly as I know how, if you want more of God, you will be unashamed of what Christians have stood staunchly for during the last two thousand years. Don't be ashamed of what you know the Bible teaches.

## Walking in the light

"If we walk in the light, as he is in the light, we have fellowship with one another, and the blood of Jesus his Son cleanses us from all sin" (1 John 1:7). Begin by walking in the truth—wherever it leads—even if it means having to give up cherished ideas that you discovered were unfounded in the Bible. Jesus said He was the "light of the world" (John 8:12). He said, "I am the way, and *the truth*, and the life" (John 14:6, emphasis added). He sent the Holy Spirit, who is the "Spirit of truth" (John 14:17). Jesus said to Pilate, "Everyone who is of the truth listens to my voice" (John 18:37).

But walking in the light also includes accepting God's will for your life—your personal life, your private life. God wants *you*. As you seek Him, you will sooner or later come across the need to change. It almost always requires going outside your comfort zone!

I made a pivotal decision in May 1982. As some of my readers know, I invited Arthur Blessitt to preach at Westminster Chapel. My motive was to have a chance to get close to him. I saw him as the nearest to being like Jesus of anyone I had met. But he said something I did not anticipate: "We need to get on the streets and talk to people about Jesus."

I thought, "Oh dear." It was not why I called him. But of course I went along with it.

But then came another hard decision: Would I do it without Arthur after he left London for another place? On a Friday night in May 1982 I had a vision of a pilot light—one that never goes out, as in a cooker or oven. I knew at that moment that I had to become a *personal soul winner*. Until then I thought I was doing my duty as a soul winner by faithfully preaching the gospel from the pulpit. I was to discover it is easier to preach from the pulpit than to give out gospel tracts between Buckingham Palace and Victoria station. Yes. And I also knew what I *had to do*— and our Pilot Light ministry was born.

In a word, I walked in the light God gave me. I now believe that had I not walked in the light at that time, God would have put me to one side—and made me yesterday's man. I am so thankful that by His grace I took the huge step to keep up ministering to people on a one-to-one basis. I have kept it up from that day to this.

For some, *walking in the light* will refer to doctrine. To some, it will mean dipping into their wallets—like tithing. To others, it will mean practicing total forgiveness toward their enemies—utterly letting them off the hook. To some, it will mean a change of job, or a change of company, or a change of diet or drink. To some, it might even be going into the ministry—or to a mission field in a strange country. To some, it could mean the willingness to speak or pray in tongues. To others, it could mean having to climb down from a hard position they took against a certain teaching or ministry.

Walking in the light of God as revealed by the Holy Spirit builds a superstructure of gold, silver, and precious stones. Whatever the price you have to pay—reputation, embarrassment, or inconvenience—it is worth it! You won't be sorry here on earth; you will be so glad for it at the judgment seat of Christ.

**Desiring earnestly the greater gifts (1 Cor. 12:31, NIV)**

This verse is probably needed today for Word people more than Spirit people. As some of my readers know, I hold that there has been a silent divorce in the church generally of the Word and the Spirit. When there is a divorce, some children stay with the mother, and some with the father. In this divorce you have those on the Word side— rightly emphasizing Bible exposition, the gospel, and sound theology—as justification by faith alone and the sovereignty of God. "What we need is solid doctrine," they would say. Those on the Spirit side rightly emphasize the Book of Acts, signs, wonders, and miracles, with the gifts of the Spirit in operation. "What we need is power," they would say.

My view: we need both; the simultaneous combination will result in spontaneous combustion.

Generally speaking, Word people emphasize the fruit of the Spirit, as in Galatians 5:22–23. Spirit people tend to emphasize the gifts of the Spirit, as in 1 Corinthians 12:8– 10. Surely we need both!

But there is often a problem for many Word people—the issue of speaking or praying in tongues. It is my view that there would never be a cessationist teaching were it not for the gift of tongues. Speaking in tongues causes the stigma. Cessationism is the teaching that the miraculous "ceased" after the era of the apostles. There is no scripture for this— none. But some are adamant about it and turn their prejudices into dogma and claim that God Himself decided the gifts ceased long ago. What sheer nonsense. And yet nobody would be against gifts such as wisdom, prophecy, or the miraculous. Because Paul inserts "tongues" into his list, many people get uneasy.

"But," say some of the Word people, "Paul said to desire earnestly the 'greater gifts,' and surely the greater gifts would be wisdom, faith, knowledge, etc." They are quick to point out that tongues is at "the bottom of the list and therefore the least important."

Granted. But I answer, "Be willing to *start at the bottom* if you want more of God!" There is hardly a greater stigma for many Christians today than the matter of tongues. Would you not be willing to bear *any* stigma if bearing the offense meant more of God?

Sadly I fear some will not consider speaking in tongues. They will resist it to the end. Some Word people hide behind any exegesis or doctrinal principle that will give them a loophole so they don't have to speak in tongues!

Here's the deal: speaking in tongues is the only gift of the Spirit that challenges your pride. That is where the water hits the wheel.

Think about it, dear reader. I agree: "Do we all have the ability to speak in unknown languages?...Of course not!" (1 Cor. 12:30, NLT). But I would have thought you must be willing to do so. And to become vulnerable and not rush for loopholes that might exempt you. For some, this could be the sticking point whether you proceed in your quest to get more of God. A friend of mine who studied at Princeton under Dr. Bruce Metzger asked him a question. (Dr. Metzger was possibly the greatest Greek scholar of the twentieth century.) The question to him was, "Did Paul mean praying in tongues when he wrote about praying with groanings that cannot be uttered in Romans 8:26–27?" Metzger replied, "Of course Paul meant that." Dr. Metzger was a Presbyterian and probably a cessationist but had enough integrity and objectivity to admit this to my friend.

## Soul winning

"Whoever captures souls is wise" (Prov. 11:30). Have you ever wondered why God blessed Billy Graham? Have you ever wondered why God blessed the Gideons, Jews for Jesus, Arthur Blessitt, or D. James Kennedy and the Coral Ridge Presbyterian Church of Fort Lauderdale, Florida? A common thread runs right through these men and organizations: they have been soul winners. That's it. Their focus was singular: the desire to see people converted to Jesus Christ.

In the days that we were in our greatest trial at Westminster Chapel—when six of our twelve deacons turned against me—there was the possibility that I could have been thrown out. The entire ordeal centered on one cause of it all: *an increased intensity in evangelism.* Had we never invited Arthur Blessitt, there would never have been a problem with the deacons who turned against our ministry. Had Arthur Blessitt never got us out into the streets of Westminster, there would never have been an uproar among the traditional members. It is true that some in the chapel did not like singing choruses or the old hymns. It is true that some saw my giving of an appeal as going against the practice of Dr. Martyn Lloyd-Jones.

But had we never begun our Pilot Light ministry, the devil would not have been stirred up.

During the height of the controversy (from April 1982 to January 1985) half of the deacons were determined to oust me from being the minister of Westminster Chapel. During that time my old friend Harry Kilbride told me again and again that I would survive because the entire issue was connected directly to the reason God sent His Son into the world to die on a cross—namely, for souls to be saved. Harry always knew we would survive. Harry knew that God would stand by me for that alone, if for no other reason.

I have thought about that a lot. After all, *the reason* that Jesus died on the cross was to save the world. It was all about evangelism—soul winning. "Follow me, and I will make you fishers of men" (Matt. 4:19). That was the *only* reason Arthur Blessitt got us out on the streets; it was to talk to people about where they would spend eternity. I reckon that Arthur Blessitt has led more people to Christ on a one-to-one basis than any human being in history. As I mentioned, when he came to spend a total of six weeks preaching at Westminster Chapel, he said to me, "We need to get out into the streets." That did not thrill me. But I honored Arthur and went along with him. It is what led to the most trouble but equally led to the fullest sense of joy and liberty we had known at the Chapel. Not that revival came. Perhaps a touch. But we were far, far better off than we were in the years preceding his coming to us—when we merely followed tradition.

My own life was never to be the same after those days.

I learned how to witness to passersby in Buckingham Gate. I also became a personal soul winner. I don't know how many were genuinely converted over the thirty-five years since, but I suppose I have led a thousand or more to pray the Sinner's Prayer—whether on trains, on planes, in taxis, or in people's homes. There will be heads of state in heaven from this one-to-one soul winning. There will be ordinary people in heaven for the same reason. Most of all, my hunger for more of God has increased because I became a soul winner. This is to say nothing about insights given me by the Spirit of God that led to the books I have written, beginning with *God Meant It for Good*.

I would appeal to you who read these lines to apply these words to yourself. It may be *way* outside your comfort zone, but I will bluntly ask you, Have you personally led a soul to Christ? Do you talk to people about Jesus and their need to be saved—do you? Your own getting more of God could be attached to this very matter. It won't do to compensate for this lack of witnessing—such as by going on a fast or increasing your giving, as significant as these sacrifices are. Soul winning is without a doubt building your superstructure with gold, silver, and precious stones.

Don't forget Paul's word to Philemon: "I pray that the sharing of your faith may become effective for the full knowledge of every good thing that is in us for the sake of Christ" (Philem. 6).

## Sexual purity

A number of years ago when I was at Spring Harvest in the UK, I listened to another speaker and was then asked to minister to some of the people who came forward after his sermon. He spoke on the subject of deliverance. When I think of that subject, my mind goes to spiritual warfare, the area of the demonic, and so on. But to my surprise, of the several people I counseled, *every single one of them*—from a single young man to married couples to a vicar's wife—came to talk about their sex problems. They ranged from masturbation to impotence to frigidity to infidelity. I had dealt with these issues in the vestry at Westminster Chapel, but I was not prepared to deal with them that evening. All of them needed prayer for deliverance pertaining to their sexual lives.

Sexual purity is an issue for many, from high-profile Christian leaders to Roman Catholic priests to single Christians to people in the churches who have little or no profile. It is on nearly everybody's minds—these days more than ever. It is the way Hollywood thrives and the way TV programs get ratings; it sells products of nearly every kind and divides families. Billy Graham once said to a friend of mine that it seems the devil gets 75 percent of God's best people through sexual temptation.

There is nothing that brings disgrace upon the name of Jesus Christ and the reputation of the church like sexual sin. Newspapers and magazines love it when a Christian leader falls; they milk the story for all it's worth. The more Christians give in to sexual temptation, the more the world can say, "They are no different from us."

"Sex was not born in Hollywood but at the throne of grace," as I remember Dr. Clyde Narramore (1916–2015) used to say. Martin Luther is often quoted as saying that

God uses sex to drive a man to marriage, ambition to drive a man to service, and fear to drive a man to faith.[5] But nowadays it is rare for a person to wait until he or she is married to have sex. Sadly this is more and more true with Christians as well. I know of too many pastors and vicars who sweep this issue under the carpet lest they run off single Christians who are sleeping with each other. One very prominent Evangelical preached a hard sermon on maintaining sexual purity until marriage but took it down from his website within a week because so many complained and threatened to stop coming to church.

Masturbation is the chief sin of many Christians and also many ministers. Dr. Martyn Lloyd-Jones told me he has had "hundreds" of preachers come to him with this issue. Masturbation is by comparison less serious than the physical act of fornication or adultery. We usually define *fornication* as a single person having sex outside of marriage; *adultery* applies to married people being unfaithful. Lusting is breaking Jesus' interpretation of the seventh commandment: "You shall not commit adultery" (Exod. 20:14). Jesus said that to even look at a person lustfully is to commit adultery in the "heart" (Matt. 5:28), which is why watching or reading pornography is sinful. You may think that watching pornography is innocent since "it isn't hurting anybody." But it has the effect of breaking down marriages because people will sometimes find pornography more exciting than the physical act. And it may lead to impotence in many young men for the same reason.

You may ask, "Can a person maintain sexual purity if he or she gives in to masturbation but does not commit the outward act of fornication?" I honestly don't know. I don't want to be unfair. It could fall under the category of working out your salvation with "fear and trembling" (Phil. 2:12). The same would apply to gay sex. One is not to be condemned for his or her proclivity, but a gay person must resist temptation as any robust heterosexual person must also do. I deal with this in my book *God Is for the Homosexual* (out of print).

Resisting temptation to have sex outside of heterosexual marriage is helping to build a superstructure of gold, silver, and precious stones. In a word, if you want more of God, you will prove it by resisting sexual temptation. It wasn't easy for Joseph when Potiphar's wife flirted with him. We know that because he "fled" (Gen. 39:12). It was not easy for him. It promised to be the "perfect affair": she would not tell her husband, and nobody who knew Joseph (back in Canaan) would ever find out. But he said no! The angels said yes! He could not have known that he was earmarked to be the prime minister of Egypt one day.

God has a plan for your life—whether you are young or old. Don't throw it away by giving in to sexual temptation. God also wants you to finish well. Don't let sexual impurity disrupt your walk with God. It is *so* not worth it.

**Perseverance in faith**

It is essential to persevere to the end if you want to build a superstructure of gold, silver, and precious stones. I am acutely aware that well-meaning, capable people teach that not persevering to the end means you will go to hell when you die because you were never converted.

I certainly know why they believe this. But I am personally convinced there are those who have been truly converted who, for some reason, give up from extreme discouragement, fail to resist temptation, or fall away like those described in Hebrews 6:4–6:

> It is impossible, in the case of those who have once been enlightened, who have tasted the heavenly gift, and have shared in the Holy Spirit, and have tasted the goodness of the word of God and the powers of the age to come, and then have fallen away, to restore them again to repentance, since they are crucifying once again the Son of God to their own harm and holding him up to contempt.

The writer of Hebrews was comparing those Jewish Christians—truly converted—to the ancient Israelites whom God swore in His wrath would not enter His rest (Heb. 3:11). The "rest"—or Promised Land (land of Canaan)—is what they forfeited. They are like those who do not build a superstructure of gold, silver, and precious stones. They will be saved by fire but lose their reward (1 Cor. 3:14–15).

I am certainly *not* saying that all who make a profession of faith or get baptized are saved. Not at all. But I expect to see those Israelites who kept the Passover and crossed the Red Sea in heaven. Most of them sadly did not please God (1 Cor. 10:5). God swore in His wrath that they would not enter into the Promised Land. Hebrews 6:4–6 refers to saved people—like the Israelites in Moses' day—who do not come into their inheritance, hence lose their reward. For further study, see *Are You Stone Deaf to the Spirit or Rediscovering God?*—my whole treatment of Hebrews 6.

These things said, Christians who are truly saved and who, for some reason, don't finish well will not receive a reward. I repeat, it is entirely possible that many of these are *professing* Christians who are not born again, and when they die, they will be eternally lost. I happen to believe that some who are saved are not completely delivered from bad habits—or they let God down for some reason—and will receive no reward at the judgment seat of Christ. I'm afraid people like this show that they did not want more of God. And yet I must add, I am not their judge. Nor are you! Let us remember Paul's words:

> Therefore do not pronounce judgment before the time, before the Lord comes, who will bring to light the things now hidden in darkness and will disclose the purposes of the heart. Then each one will receive his commendation from God.
>
> —1 CORINTHIANS 4:5

I paraphrase Luther's previously mentioned statement: there will be some who receive a reward at the judgment seat of Christ that I thought would surely have no reward; there will be those who do not receive a reward at the judgment seat of Christ that I thought would surely receive a reward. But the greatest surprise of all will be if I receive a reward at the judgment seat of Christ.

In 1 Corinthians 9:27 Paul wasn't sure he had secured such a reward:

> But I discipline my body and keep it under con-
> trol, lest after preaching to others I myself should
> be disqualified.

That's me. Right now. Though I am an old man, I may
have years left. I cannot lose my salvation, but I *could*
come short of my inheritance—or reward. That was Paul
in approximately AD 55. But in AD 65, in his last epistle—
waiting to be executed in Rome at any moment—he could
claim to have what he wanted!

> For I am already being poured out as a drink
> offering, and the time of my departure has come. I
> have fought the good fight, I have finished the race,
> I have kept the faith. Henceforth there is laid up
> for me the crown of righteousness, which the Lord,
> the righteous judge, will award to me on that day,
> and not only to me but also to all who have loved
> his appearing.
>
> —2 TIMOTHY 4:6–8

## EXAMPLES OF WOOD, HAY, AND STRAW

### Unsound teaching

There are degrees of heresy (false doctrine), and it is not
always easy to draw the line. If we came up with a scale of
one to ten, with one being extreme heresy and ten being
harmless heresy, it would still be hard to know which
number to assign to all the teachings we could mention.

Take Karl Barth (1886–1968), for example. He is regarded
by many as the greatest theologian since Jonathan Edwards.
But without a doubt he was a universalist. He left no room

in his theology for a person going to hell. His teaching is dangerous but perhaps mostly because he lured decent Evangelicals away from orthodoxy to his views. Why did they accept his views? Primarily, I think, because he believed in the virgin birth of Christ and His resurrection from the dead. He also professed to be a Reformed theologian, often quoting John Calvin, which made young Evangelicals feel "safe" with him—at first. Those who became Barthians rarely stayed Barthians. That is another story, but my point is this: if one is to believe J. I. Packer, who said that Barth was "on the side of the angels" at the end of the day, one would also say Barth was a Christian and will be in heaven. After all, according to Romans 10:9–10, Barth was saved. But Barthianism is by no means a harmless heresy; it is dangerous.

Take Rudolf Bultmann (1884–1976). He is the architect of what he called "demythologizing." The idea is that the Bible is full of myths—traditional stories that may or may not be true. Whether it be the virgin birth, Jesus walking on water, or the resurrection of Jesus from the dead, these are at best "myths," he said. But not to worry; we can learn from these myths, says Bultmann. God wants us to walk on water as Peter did! Never mind that Peter may or may not (probably not) have literally walked on water, but we can derive help by realizing we can do impossible things! The truth is, Bultmann did not believe in the truth of the Bible for a minute! But he taught we could learn wonderful things from the myths. So sad. In my opinion, a person like this could not be saved. What about a person who was truly converted but reads Bultmann and becomes excited over his teaching? Has he lost his salvation? Or was he never saved? How could a genuinely saved person imbibe such heresy as Bultmannism? I want to believe it is possible but not likely. I am not the judge. And yet there are innocent Christians who sit under the teaching of those who had been influenced by Bultmann who lack discernment. I would not want to say these people are not saved.

As for dangerous heresy (Bultmann, Barth) as opposed to harmless heresy (those who do not believe in sovereign grace and believe you can lose your salvation), such people may well be saved. John Wesley (1703–1791), who taught Christian perfection and popularized Arminianism (believing in free will and the possibility of losing your salvation after being truly converted), was a godly man. His opponent was his old friend George Whitefield (1714–1770), who upheld his belief in predestination. Someone reportedly asked Wesley if he anticipated seeing Whitefield in heaven. Wesley's reply: "No....He will be so close to the throne of God and I so far away that I will not be able to see him!"[6] Lovely comment!

When I preached in a church in the early sixties, I got into trouble for stating that Jesus is God. When I look back on that era, I wonder if people with those beliefs could have been saved. Probably not, but I am not their judge.

The teaching of open theism (God does not know the future, is enriched by His creation, and looks to us for input) is a dangerous heresy. But I happen to believe that some who adhere to this—at least friends of mine I know quite well—are converted. As for "hyper-grace" teaching—that saved people don't need to confess their sins since

Jesus already paid for them on the cross—I accept that these people are saved. But oh my! What awful teaching!

Unsound doctrine is like wood, hay, and straw. When Martin Luther (1483–1546) called James "an epistle of straw,"[7] he was referring to the "straw" in 1 Corinthians 3:12. It was a terrible thing to say! But does this mean that Luther did not truly convert?

The truth is, I suspect there is a bit of wood, hay, and straw in all of us! The fire will burn up what is not gold, silver, or precious stones. How God will determine who gets a reward and who doesn't in the light of this teaching is not my problem! God will judge.

I am sure of this: God hates unsound teaching. We need to get it right doctrinally. I want to build a superstructure of the purest theology possible! How we assess the Bible and what it teaches must be done with fear and trembling.

**Holding grudges**

In this chapter I shall merely introduce an essential feature in the building of the superstructure with gold, silver, and precious gems. It is in fact so important that I shall devote a whole chapter to this. What follows here is but an introduction to this essential aspect in the super-structure. "For if you forgive others their trespasses, your heavenly Father will also forgive you, but if you do not forgive others their trespasses, neither will your Father forgive your trespasses" (Matt. 6:14–15). This verse is from the Sermon on the Mount and immediately follows Jesus' teaching of what we know as the Lord's Prayer. In the Lord's Prayer are these words: "Forgive us our debts, as we also have forgiven our debtors" (Matt. 6:12). Luke's version says, "Forgive us our sins, for we ourselves forgive everyone who is indebted to us" (Luke 11:4).

We hold a grudge because we cannot forgive. A grudge is a feeling of bitterness, anger, or resentment owing to being hurt. It is as natural as breathing. No one needs to teach us how to do it; it comes without training or education. A child learns to feel resentment from his or her earliest days. The most natural thing in the world is to want to get even with the person who has hurt you. You want revenge. You want that person to get his or her comeuppance.

That said, what is wrong with it? The answer: it grieves the Holy Spirit. After Paul said for us not to grieve the Holy Spirit of God, with whom we are sealed for the day of redemption (Eph. 4:30), the very next thing he said was:

> Let all bitterness and wrath and anger and clamor
> and slander be put away from you, along with all
> malice. Be kind to one another, tenderhearted, for-
> giving one another, as God in Christ forgave you.
> —EPHESIANS 4:31–32

With this there is good news and bad news. First, the good news: when we grieve the Holy Spirit, it does not mean we lose our salvation. After all, said Paul, we are "sealed for the day of redemption" (Eph. 4:30)! That is good news.

It is equally true that forgiveness is not a prerequisite to being a Christian. If it were, no one would be saved. Jesus, in the Lord's Prayer, inserted the petition "Forgive us our debts" (Matt. 6:12; see also Luke 11:4) because He knew that we all sin every day. He put this most gracious provision in His pattern prayer for us. This sin, debt, or trespass almost always implies our weakness in the area of forgiving one another, so Jesus added that we forgive those who sin against us.

That said, the Lord's Prayer has probably made more liars out of people than any document in history. (Because they've prayed that they forgive others when they haven't.) But we cannot blame the Lord; we must blame ourselves— or not pray the Lord's Prayer. And yet not praying puts us in disobedience because Jesus commanded us to pray this prayer (Matt. 6:9; Luke 11:2).

You might say that Jesus said, "If you do not forgive others their trespasses, neither will your Father forgive your trespasses" (Matt. 6:15), which is absolutely true. But this warning is *not* in reference to salvation. The Lord's Prayer is not a prayer for how to become a Christian. It addresses those already in the family. But some will say, "This shows you can lose your salvation if you don't forgive people their sins." I reply, "If that is the case, nobody would be saved. Can you say that *you* never have a problem forgiving others?"

Jesus gave the Lord's Prayer to those already in the family of God. It is a prayer that we might inherit the kingdom of heaven. All Christians are called to come into their inheritance. Some do; some don't. Those who do come into their inheritance practice forgiving others; those who don't refuse to forgive others—and hold a grudge. This concept is so important that I will return to it later in this book. But for now I am compelled to say if you want more of God, you must prove it by totally forgiving those who have sinned against you. It is possibly the toughest challenge of all.

## Grumbling

Grumbling is the polar opposite of gratitude. If you want an idea of how much God hates ingratitude, read these verses that described the previously mentioned generation of the children of Israel who forfeited their inheritance:

> Now these things took place as examples for us, that we might not desire evil as they did. Do not be idolaters as some of them were; as it is written, "The people sat down to eat and drink and rose up to play." We must not indulge in sexual immorality as some of them did, and twenty-three thousand fell in a single day. We must not put Christ to the test, as some of them did and were destroyed by serpents, nor grumble, as some of them did and were destroyed by the Destroyer.
>
> —1 CORINTHIANS 10:6–10

Note the sins mentioned: idolatry, sexual immorality, testing God, and grumbling. Because grumbling is not nearly as scandalous as sexual immorality, we might easily underestimate how much God hates it. Yet it is equal to sexual immorality in His sight. This by itself should give us pause. Also remember that in Romans 1:18–32—those verses list the most horrible sins imaginable under the sun—are these words: "For although they knew God, they did not honor him as God or give thanks to him" (v. 21).

I got an unexpected wake-up call one day when I was preaching on Philippians 4:6:

> Do not be anxious about anything, but in everything by prayer and supplication with thanksgiving let your requests be made known to God.

For some reason my whole life, as it were, came before me right in the middle of my sermon. I was convicted of unthankfulness as I reiterated Paul's words "with thanksgiving" in Philippians 4:6. I was not prepared for this. But I was shaken so much that I quietly pleaded with the Lord to help me finish the sermon quickly so I could get to my desk in the vestry and fall on my face in repentance before Him. When I went into the vestry and shut the door—making sure I would be alone for a while, I began to repent as I had not done in many, many years. The Holy Spirit brought to my mind the many things God had done for me—huge things that I should not have overlooked. I thought I heard the Lord say, "You are from Kentucky. Are you thankful that I put you where you are?"

I replied, "Lord, You know I'm thankful."

"But you didn't tell Me," He replied.

I could mention many things in this paragraph—huge things, the most obvious things for which I should have been extremely grateful. I would say, "But Lord, You know I'm thankful."

He kept saying, "But you didn't tell Me." I felt utterly ashamed.

I made a vow that day—a vow I have kept: to be a thankful man from that day forward. Starting the very next morning, when I went through my journal, I began thanking God for every single thing from the previous day for which I was thankful. It takes less than twenty seconds! But I make sure I tell Him.

There are three rules I offer: (1) God loves gratitude. (2) God hates ingratitude. (3) Gratitude must be taught. This wake-up call led me to teach gratitude to my congregation. I realized that as Paul needed to teach sanctification to his converts, so too must one teach gratitude. After all, sanctification is the doctrine of gratitude.

A couple of years ago Mayo Clinic said in its monthly bulletin (which I receive) that researchers had clinically proved *thankful people live longer*. How about that as a motive?

On one occasion Jesus healed ten lepers. Only one came back to say thank you. The first thing Jesus said was, "Were not ten cleansed? Where are the nine?" (Luke 17:17). God loves gratitude. He notices and hates ingratitude.

Grumbling is a sure sign of ingratitude. I lovingly say to you, if you knew how much God hates ingratitude, you would *stop it*!

Christians who are complainers may not realize it, but they are building a superstructure of wood, hay, and straw. Don't do that. Stop carping. Stop murmuring. Stop grumbling. Stop complaining.

I offer this acrostic that might be helpful. Try to remember before you speak to ask, "Will what I say meet another person's NEED?" NEED is an acrostic, which I will explain. Everyone you meet has a need. All of us are needy. It is so sweet when someone says what meets our need at the moment—whether a compliment or helpful advice. Therefore, ask these questions before you speak:

- **"Is it *necessary*?"** In other words, must I really say this? Is it necessary to say what I am about to say? If not, I won't say it! Remember too, when words are many, sin is not absent (Prov. 10:19). Say what needs to be said—and no more. It will save you much sorrow and regret.

- **"Is it *emancipating*?"** Do you realize that 100 percent of people you will meet today have a guilt problem over something? Say what will set them free! That is what Jesus did with His words—He set people free. "Where the Spirit of the Lord is, there is freedom" (2 Cor. 3:17).

- **"Is it *energizing*?"** There are two kinds of people: the energizers and the complainers. Don't you dread seeing the complainer walking up to you again? You know what he is going to say. It is draining of energy and morale. But that person who energizes you, saying what builds you up, is so uplifting!

- **"Is it *dignifying*?"** Jesus gave people dignity. That is what He did for Mary Magdalene, out of whom He cast seven devils (Luke 8:2). She was a prostitute, but Jesus gave her dignity. The woman found in adultery dreaded

what Jesus would say, but He said, "Neither
do I condemn you; go, and from now on sin
no more" (John 8:11).

*Necessary, emancipating, energizing,* and *dignifying* =
NEED. All Jesus ever said met one's *need*. It flows out of
a life of gratitude, one devoid of grumbling. Grumbling is
sheer wood, hay, and straw in the superstructure you and
I are to build.

## Gossiping

Gossiping is listening to reports about other people's
private lives that might be unkind, disapproving, or not
true. It may be about a public figure—a movie star or
politician—who has fallen, gotten found out about, or
had terrible things happen to him or her. It may be about
someone who has become your enemy. Gossip often
thrives on jealousy. Take jealousy out of the picture, and
gossip tends to stop altogether.

Gossip is not necessary. If the acrostic just mentioned
is followed, there would be no gossip. It does not meet
anyone's need. What is more, it negatively affects anyone
seeking to get more of God. "The words of a whisperer are
like delicious morsels; they go down into the inner parts of
the body" (Prov. 18:8). I'm sorry to say I know exactly what
that means. I have experienced this. Too many times. First,
once we choose to listen to gossip, we become insatiable. As
"whoever loves money never has enough" (Eccles. 5:10, NIV),
so too with gossip; once you begin listening to gossip, you
never get enough of it. Like morsels that do not satisfy but
are tasty, it sinks to our lowest motives and wishes. It leaves

one empty. Unsatisfied. Unclean. I dare say that if you and I are not earnestly pursuing knowing God more deeply and having more of Him, we will hardly be aware of it when we are engaging in gossip. It is so much a part of life that we tend to take no notice of it. It sells magazines and is often the thread that holds a relationship together. There are news networks that keep their ratings up by constant propaganda, reporting unflattering things about their political enemies. I fear some people who often see each other would have no relationship at all if gossip were not the main ingredient in their being together. "What's the latest?" I can hear people saying. They often want information that will tickle their insecure egos—information, whether true or not, that makes the enemy look bad.

Gossip may be a report of true facts and events. It is not always rumor or secondhand information. In any case gossip almost always thrives on jealousy. As envy "makes the bones rot" (Prov. 14:30), so gossip robs us of personal dignity. Whether the report is true or not, a lover of gossip wants more rumors. Whether true or not, there is something about our sinful nature that gets excited if there is bad news regarding someone we are jealous of.

> Do not rejoice when your enemy falls, and let not your heart be glad when he stumbles, lest the LORD see it and be displeased, and turn away his anger from him.
>
> —PROVERBS 24:17–18

How does that make you feel? If you rejoice in another's bad news, God will take notice and may even send judgment on you! Paul told us to "weep with those who weep" and "rejoice with those who rejoice" (Rom. 12:15). It is not too hard to find someone who will weep with you. A true friend—rare—is one who will rejoice with you. But gossip is rejoicing over another's bad news.

There are different kinds of gossiping. According to a blog called *Going by Faith*, here are some types of gossiping:

1. Spreading rumors about someone with the purpose of damaging his or her reputation. We are to "rid" ourselves of slander (Col. 3:8, NIV). James said, "Do not speak evil against one another" (Jas. 4:11).

2. "Dishin' the dirt"—that is, sharing the "juicy info" you heard about someone. "Whoever goes about slandering reveals secrets; therefore do not associate with a simple babbler" (Prov. 20:19).

3. Repeating rumors. You hear something that's not good, nor is it confirmed as being true. But you repeat it, hoping it's true.

4. Telling "not-really-joking jokes." It is when you take part of a truth and turn it into a joke that makes others question someone's character. "Many a true word is spoken in jest," as it has been said.

5. Planting a seed. We reap what we sow. When we plant a seed that could cause division, even the mere dropping of an

uncomplimentary word—whether true or not—that can be divisive. "A dishonest man spreads strife, and a whisperer separates close friends" (Prov. 16:28).

6. Whispering innuendos. This is saying something that will cause someone to suspect the worst of a situation—as when a man gives a helpful lift in his car to a woman, and afterward tongues wag. This is why Billy Graham never spent a night away from home without his friend T. W. Wilson in the same hotel room. I remember offering to drive Joyce Meyer only two blocks, but she made a woman get in the car with her!

7. "Got-this-all-wrong" gossiping. This is when "you admit you probably got it wrong, but spread it anyway." It sounds exciting if true, so you tell it.[8]

Gossiping is something to avoid entirely, even if it's true. One of the things I learned from William Perkins (1558–1602): don't believe the devil, even when he tells the truth. So too it is with gossip. The breath of Satan is behind it. It will sap us spiritually. When you are tempted to gossip, treat it like a rattlesnake. Have nothing to do with it. Keep yourself pure from this sort of thing; it does the opposite of edifying and energizing and instead drains you of clean, wholesome, and godly motivation.

When you are tempted to listen to or spread gossip, ask, "Will this make me want more of God?"

# Chapter 7

# DIGNIFYING THE TRIAL

*Count it all joy, my brothers, when you
meet trials of various kinds.*
—JAMES 1:2

I T's A TRIVIAL story—at least to you, no doubt. But
to me, silly though it will sound, it was utterly life
changing. Some of you will recall the story—and will
forgive me for referring to it here.

It was in the summer of 1979. We were in Kissimmee,
Florida, to take our children to Disney World. However, I
was not looking forward to Disney World but to a nearby
pizza parlor that served the best pizza I had ever tasted. I

couldn't wait to eat it again—that is, if it would be like the one I ate during the previous summer there.

My memory of that pizza kept me looking forward to this vacation for an entire year. The moment finally arrived, and with great anticipation we ordered the pizza. But after forty-five minutes my patience was wearing thin. When our server came back and asked, "What was that order again?" I realized he had forgotten our order! I was not at my best (to show my mastery of British understatement). I lost my temper.

When the pizzas were finally ready, we headed to the car to take them back to our hotel. It began raining—rain like you have not seen. It drenched us. We could not see five feet in front of the car.

When we got to the hotel, Louise and the kids grabbed their pizza and quickly darted into the hotel room. Intending to follow them, I reached for my pizza and...stepped into a foot of water as the rain came down on the brown paper bag with the pizza inside. The next thing I saw was my pizza floating on the water like a little battleship covered with pepperoni, mushrooms, sausage, peppers, tomatoes, and cheese.

Soaked and frustrated, I explained to the family that I had to return to the pizza place. Disinterested in my plight, they had already found a television program they wanted to see. But I had to face the same server.

The rain stopped. It was only a five-minute drive back to the pizza parlor. But in those five minutes the Holy Spirit graciously did a job on me. I began to think of a sermon I had been preparing to preach on James 1:2 (quoted previously). "Either what I will preach is true, or it isn't," I said to myself. "I must count this awkward moment *joy*. I must dignify this trial." Yes. That is when I came up with the phrase "dignify the trial."

To finish the story, I went back to the pizza restaurant and approached the same server on bended knee, telling him what happened. He was surprisingly gracious and did not charge me for the second order!

But what I remember most was the increased level of joy all day long at Disney World the next day. Whether riding on Space Mountain or drinking cold grape juice in the hot sun, all I could think about was the high level of God's presence with me—the privilege of dignifying the trial. I knew I would never be the same again. And I wasn't to be.

That does not mean I am just like Jesus every time a trial suddenly hits me. But I can say it has made a big difference in me from what I used to be before the summer of 1979, when—I am ashamed to tell you—I was always complaining, murmuring, and grumbling when disruptions blocked my plans or inconvenienced my day. I do pray that this chapter will somehow have the same life-changing effect on you as the pizza incident had on me.

The main thing I learned from my pizza experience and the passage in James 1:2 is this: every trial is a gift from God. It is a present from Him, an invitation, one far more important to you than being invited to meet the president, the queen, or some celebrity you might want to talk about. This invitation has to do with your moral character. It is why God gives you trials—sometimes a small one, sometimes a huge one. He entrusts you with them because they come with invitations to get closer to God and to get more of Him.

Do you want more of God? I can guarantee one of the best ways to do this is by dignifying the trial He puts in your path. One of my favorite hymns is "Like a River Glorious." It includes this verse:

> Ev'ry joy or trial falleth from above,
> Traced upon our dial by the Sun of Love;
> We may trust Him fully all for us to do;
> They who trust Him wholly find Him wholly true.[1]
> —Frances R. Havergal (1836–1879)

The Greek word *peirasmos* means testing, trial, or temptation.[2] Because these words can be used interchangeably, the context should dictate whether we translate *peirasmos* as temptation or trial.

It is interesting that the author of "Like a River Glorious" uses the phrase "falleth from above." A trial—like joy—comes from God. He is the architect of both. This is why James tells us to consider it all joy if we *fall* into any trial. It may well lead you to the same place as a ninety-year-old saint who told me, "I have been serving the Lord for so long now that I can hardly tell the difference between a blessing and a trial."

## Don't Go Looking for Trials

Since we should count a trial "joy," one might hastily conclude that we should go out looking for trials in order to have more joy! Don't do that—ever.

It is essential to understand this. It is why we should pray the Lord's Prayer daily, noting the petition "Lead us not *into* temptation" (Matt. 6:13, emphasis added). As I explain in my book *The Lord's Prayer,* this petition is the most difficult part of Jesus' prayer. The implication is that God Himself might lead us into temptation. Wrong. This is possibly why James, the brother of Jesus, made a big point of this in his general epistle, which we are partially examining in this chapter.

> Let no one say when he is tempted, "I am being tempted by God," for God cannot be tempted with evil, and he himself tempts no one. But each person is tempted when he is lured and enticed by his own desire. Then desire when it has conceived gives birth to sin, and sin when it is fully grown brings forth death.
>
> —JAMES 1:13–15

God will never—ever—tempt us. That said, He may well *test* us. Even though the Greek word is the same, there is a huge difference in the way this word is to be understood. We are told that "God tested Abraham" (Gen. 22:1). It was a setup: God wanted to see if Abraham really and truly feared Him. This test was for Abraham's benefit, not God's; God already knew what was in Abraham's heart. But Abraham needed to see for himself what he would do in such a situation.

God may providentially lead us in a manner that *allows* us to be tried or tested in order for us to see what we are. Such, therefore, is a test. God is giving us an exam to see what we know! That said, we should never say that God directly tempts us.

Michael Eaton has been very helpful here; he said we should stress the word *into*, that we should pray that God will not allow us to be "thrown in at the deep end," as it were. Trials are bound to come. Jesus assured us that in this world we would have trouble (John 16:33); however, we should not go out looking for trouble but rather pray that God will be pleased to spare us of trouble! *But if* after trying to avoid trials and praying that God will not let us be led *into* temptation or trial, we are *still* thrown into a trial, *then* we should consider it joy. This way you know God did it and you did not cause it. When you know that God is the architect of the trial you are going through, you are commanded to count the trial as joy.

Therefore, James said we could consider it all joy if we "fall into" trials or troubles (Jas. 1:2, KJV). The Greek word is *parapiptō*—to fall or fall to one side.[3] The NIV refers to facing trials, but that misses a huge point. We are not going to have more joy merely by looking at a trial; we qualify to count it all joy when we *fall into* it. In other words, it is what happens to you, not what you made happen.

On the other hand, we can all bring on trials by our own folly. Peter warned, "But let none of you suffer as a murderer or a thief or an evildoer or as a meddler" (1 Pet. 4:15). This verse shows that not all trials come from God! We can bring on our own suffering—through sin! We can also bring on persecution from being stupid—as meddlers or "busybodies" (2 Thess. 3:11; 1 Tim. 5:13). A busybody is a prying person, a gossip, a troublemaker. People like this bring on their own suffering and sometimes want to call it persecution. Those who suffer from their own lack of wisdom may experience grief, yes, but people like this need to repent before they can dignify their trials.

How then are we to understand Paul's words?

> No temptation has overtaken you that is not common to man. God is faithful, and he will not let you be tempted beyond your ability, but with the temptation he will also provide the way of escape, that you may be able to endure it.
>
> —1 CORINTHIANS 10:13

I think 1 Corinthians 10:13 is probably the first verse a new Christian should try to memorize. It is vital to our Christian growth; it also gives us insight into some of God's ways. Although *peirasmos* can rightly refer to being tempted and temptation, it is still fair to remember that the word means tested and testing too.

## SEXUAL TEMPTATION

But how do you dignify a trial when the testing is a sexual temptation? First, see it as a test from God. He wants to show you His grace. See it as a testing and certainly not Him giving you the green light to give in to sexual temptation because He permitted it. Second, you dignify a trial like this by refusing to sin. That is what Joseph did, as we saw earlier.

I remember a couple who came into the vestry of Westminster Chapel to explain why they fell into adultery. "We both prayed about it, including praying the Lord's

121

Prayer that day, and, lo and behold, we ran into each other unexpectedly and realized that God was allowing us to have each other." That is the way they *chose to see their sin*.

Joseph might have rationalized his sexual temptation regarding Potiphar's wife as being what God was providing him in his loneliness and possible anger toward God. After all, he did not ask to be living in Egypt. Joseph did not flirt with Mrs. Potiphar; she initiated the matter by chasing him. But he *chose not to sin*. He thus dignified that trial.

First Corinthians 10:13 is God's guarantee that you can resist sexual temptation—whether you are heterosexual or homosexual. You make a choice. You dignify the trial by maintaining holiness. You do not dignify the trial if you justify yourself by giving in to temptation.

First Corinthians 10:13 equally refers to any testing—grief, financial reverse, sickness, or losing your job. If you have been thrown into the deep end—a trial not of your making but what God has allowed—you qualify to dignify such a trial by refusing to blame God or complain.

## IMPUTE JOY TO THE TRIAL

Although James does not use the same Greek word in James 1:2 as does Paul in Romans 4, the application by each comes to the same thing when you compare them. James said, "*Count* it all joy." In Romans 4 our faith is *counted* as righteousness. The NIV uses the words *credited* and *count*:

What does Scripture say? "Abraham believed God, and it was credited to him as righteousness." Now to the one who works, wages are not credited as a gift but as an obligation. However, to the one who does not work but trusts God who justifies the ungodly, their faith is credited as righteousness. David says the same thing when he speaks of the blessedness of the one to whom God credits righteousness apart from works: "Blessed are those whose transgressions are forgiven, whose sins are covered. Blessed is the one whose sin the Lord will never count against them."

—ROMANS 4:3–8, NIV, EMPHASIS ADDED

The similarity is this: if we compare Paul's exposition of Abraham's faith that counted as righteousness in God's sight to the way James wants us to regard a trial, we have the same application.

- As God counted Abraham's faith as righteousness, we should regard a trial as a matter of joy.

- Abraham's faith was credited to him as righteousness, so we should credit a trial as joy.

- When we trust God, who justifies, our faith is credited as righteousness, so when we fall into a trial, we should credit it as a matter of joy.

The word *impute* summarizes it. *Impute* means put to the charge or credit of. When we transfer our trust in good works to what Jesus has done for us on the cross, God *imputes righteousness* to us. Righteousness is, therefore, put to our credit. *That is the way God sees us.* When we trust Christ's blood, God *counts* or *considers* us as righteous.

As in the case of David's word—from Psalm 32:1–2, blessed are those whose sins are not *counted* against them by God—so we should not *count* a trial as a thing of sorrow but count it as joy.

Here's the big thing: there was nothing righteous about Abraham before he believed the promise God gave to him. He was a sun worshipper. But in one stroke God saw Abraham as righteous because Abraham believed the promise that he would have an heir and have offspring as numerous as the stars in the heavens (Gen. 15:5–6). Abraham might have said to God, "Don't joke with me like that. Do you expect me—age eighty-five with a barren wife age seventy-five—to believe a word like that?" But Abraham did believe it! Yes, and God counted him as righteous.

God did not wait for Abraham to develop into a godly man—which he truly did later—to count him as righteous. God did it then and there—once for all. Likewise, you and I are not asked to wait until later—when we see the positive effect a trial has on our lives—to impute joy to it. *We are to do it now.*

Don't wait for Romans 8:28 to prove true at first. "All things work together for good to them that love God" (KJV)—yes. Absolutely. But not by tomorrow afternoon. It almost always takes a good while before we see for our-selves how the trial worked together for good.

In other words, James tells us that a trial is for our good—and we will see it clearly down the road. He is telling us to see it as good immediately and not wait for what happens down the road.

I can tell you, Romans 8:28 is true, absolutely true. But it takes time to see it outwardly and objectively. The greatest trials I had during my twenty-five years at Westminster Chapel—the best of times, the worst of times—are what I now treasure. What I honestly thought was the *worst* thing that ever happened to me I now honestly regard as the *best* thing that ever happened to me.

By the way, even my folly works together for good—eventually. Yes, when I am foolish and bring suffering on myself, that too falls into God's melting pot. He takes the bad and the ugly of our lives and turns them into a pat-tern for good. He is a gracious God. He is so good.

That said, James is telling us in James 1:2 to consider the trial as all joy—*now*. Don't wait until later when it takes no faith to believe it. Get the maximum victory when you cannot remotely see how this trial could be a good thing! That is the time James wants us to impute joy to the trial, tragedy, hurt, or reversal.

Do you want more of God? I urge you to prove this by dignifying the trial *now*.

A greater level of glory is often preceded immediately by a trial.

We shall look later at 2 Corinthians 3:18, which says that we are being changed "from one degree of glory to another."

There are peak experiences that grant us a higher level of *consciousness* of God. God grants us this to confirm we are on the right track—that we truly want more of Him. Not only that; our going from "glory to glory" *is actually getting more of God*!

However, you will find that, possibly more often than not, a closer walk with God is preceded by a trial— sometimes a small trial, sometimes an acute one. It is my own experience that when there is a satanic attack, I can mark it down; God is near! Something good is coming shortly, and this coheres with 1 Peter 5:10.

> And after you have suffered a little while, the God of all grace, who has called you to his eternal glory in Christ, will himself restore, confirm, strengthen, and establish you.

Billy Graham honored us by preaching for me at Westminster Chapel in May 1984. On the Friday preceding that he spent an hour and forty-five minutes with me. One of the things he shared with me was this: "In every crusade we have ever had, there has been an attack of the devil just before it starts. It may be a sickness or illness, it may be members of the team falling out with each other, but there is always something." He told me this because he was coming down with something that required him to go to the hospital right after our visit. He developed a nosebleed. He actually left his hospital bed and came to Westminster Chapel with a box of tissues that he kept at hand should the nosebleed worsen in the middle of his sermon! Photos of him preaching for us show his hospital

ID band on his left wrist. The point is, he felt he was under attack—not so much because he was preaching for us but because Mission England, a series of meetings that lasted for weeks, began at the chapel that evening.

When, therefore, we fall into a severe trial, and our immediate reaction is negative, we are to consider the trial a positive thing right then and there, before it has a chance to prove positive. When our immediate reaction is self-pity, we are to regard the trial as an occasion to rejoice then and there. When we are greatly disappointed when we receive bad news, we should see it as good news right then. Really? How can we do this? I answer, "If Abraham could believe what seemed at the time to be a word most preposterous as God's word, then we too should regard James' word as a word from God and impute joy to a trial."

I don't say it will be easy to do this. Nor am I saying that since the pizza incident I have been a model testimony to what I am writing in this chapter. I have failed and will possibly continue to fail more than I want to admit to you. But the difference is this: I truly know my responsibility before God, and I, therefore, tell myself I will be glad if I dignify this trial—now.

There is a good possibility that someone reading these lines at this moment is in the greatest trial of his life. Is that you? The apostle Paul described his greatest trial:

> For we do not want you to be unaware, brothers,
> of the affliction we experienced in Asia. For we
> were so utterly burdened beyond our strength that
> we despaired of life itself. Indeed, we felt that we

had received the sentence of death. But that was
to make us rely not on ourselves but on God who
raises the dead. He delivered us from such a deadly
peril, and he will deliver us. On him we have set our
hope that he will deliver us again. You also must
help us by prayer, so that many will give thanks on
our behalf for the blessing granted us through the
prayers of many.

—2 Corinthians 1:8–11

I discussed this passage with one of the greatest New
Testament scholars in the world. He told me that one can
detect a difference between the letters Paul wrote prior to
this trial—namely, 1 Corinthians, 1 and 2 Thessalonians,
Galatians, and possibly 1 Timothy and Titus—and the
letters he wrote after this trial—2 Corinthians, Romans,
Ephesians, Philippians, Colossians, and 2 Timothy. The
difference in the two groups—or periods—is not in
reliability or extent of truth; all are equally infallible. But
there is a depth in the latter group that is not as obvious
in the first group, before his great trial.

If this scholar's assessment is correct, it shows what the
trial did for Paul—it enriched him. Paul's testimony—you
read it previously—says: "that was to make us rely not on
ourselves but on God." Whereas I would have assumed
that Paul always relied on God, Paul admits that he was
not relying on God as he should have! The trial helped
him to trust God more than ever. This gives you another
reason to impute joy to a trial: what it will do for you as a
follower of Christ.

## EVERY TRIAL HAS A BUILT-IN TIMESCALE

The trials God designs for us not only are not accidental but have a timescale. Paul said that we are "destined" for trials (1 Thess. 3:3). God is at the bottom of them and also knows how much we can bear. He, therefore, has put a time limit on them. The problem is, we don't know how long they are going to last; only God knows. But it is good to know that our trials will end! We may think they will go on forever. But they will end—often suddenly. Then when the trials are over, they're over.

Here is an important thing to remember: every trial is a test from God to see whether you dignified it or complained all the way through it. It is an exam—you pass or fail. I'm sorry, but that is the way it is. If you pass, God moves you upward to a higher level of glory. This is mainly what the phrase "being transformed into the same image from one degree of glory to another" (2 Cor. 3:18) means. But this transition almost always is preceded by a trial of some sort. If you pass, the reward is *so* satisfying. It comes with supernatural peace and joy. You can tell you pass by the inner testimony of the Holy Spirit. It is what I felt at Disney World the day following my acceptance of the pizza incident as a gift from God.

But what if you fail? Nothing happens. Life goes on. And you never know what you missed by complaining throughout the trial the whole time. I know. I'm ashamed to repeat it—it is the way I reacted to blocked goals and sudden disappointments for years and years. Soon after this insight about dignifying the trial came to me, I preached on James 1:2 at Westminster Chapel. I began to realize how much joy I had missed over the years. I started to think of the spiritual progress I lost during those years. I simply had to claim Romans 8:28 and not look back. But I can tell you this: I vowed from that day in August 1979 to dignify every single trial—great or small—that came my way.

## SMALL TRIALS, SEVERE TRIALS

We now come to a most important matter. Although every trial has its built-in timescale, there are obviously degrees of testing. There are levels of feeling and hurt. Grief, for example, may last a long time. Recovering from financial reverse may take a while. Illness or disease can go on for years. So how can these kinds of trials have a built-in timescale?

The answer: God gives times of relief and refreshing along the way.

On December 29, 1963, I entered into a mental state of "unreality"—that is the best word I can think of to describe it. It came after a time of most severe rejection at a church I pastored in Ohio and rejection by my oldest mentor. I remember the day it happened. I always assumed that it would go away one day. Paul prayed three times for his "thorn in the flesh" to go away (2 Cor. 12:7–8)— and it never did. I have prayed a thousand times for mine to go. I've been prayed for by Dr. Martyn Lloyd-Jones and a hundred others. Some Charismatics said I was demon-possessed. A psychologist said I had a "psychotic break." I only know one thing: it's still there. But I can also say that there have been "times of refreshing" from the presence of the Lord (Acts 3:20). God has been with me from that hour to this—enabling me to survive as a door-to-door vacuum cleaner salesman to being the minister of Westminster Chapel. I still keep hoping it will go away. "You will bring me up again" (Ps. 71:20) is a verse I think about in this connection. But going to heaven will be better—and that may be the next thing God has in mind!

You may have had trials a thousand times worse—being abused or victimized, being crippled from a car accident, losing a spouse or child, losing your good health, being forever rejected by a friend. But you may also be able to testify that God has been right there with you. I think of two verses in the Bible in particular:

> I will not contend forever, nor will I always be angry; for the spirit would grow faint before me, and the breath of life that I made.
>
> —ISAIAH 57:16

> For he knows our frame; he remembers that we are dust.
>
> —PSALM 103:14

Yes, He knows just how much you can bear. Therefore, in the trial that seems endless, God steps in—not a minute too late, never too early, but always right on time.

Therefore, those who have permanent disabilities have a major opportunity to dignify the lengthy trial. Those who have other trials within those permanent disabilities may dignify the smaller ones too.

God is honored and glorified when we dignify His trials for us. Said Paul, "I ask you not to lose heart over what I am suffering for you, which is your glory" (Eph. 3:13). Their *glory*—think of that!

*It is your glory too.*

## WHY DIGNIFY THE TRIAL?

Dignifying the trial is what increases your faith. Dignifying the trial molds character. It shapes your perspective. It is the means of drawing you closer to God and is absolutely necessary for you to get more of God.

A trial is one way God gets our attention! We often think, "He certainly has my attention"—until we discover through trial: "He did not have my attention after all." We dignify the trial by submitting to His wisdom and find ourselves with a greater sense of God.

Faith pleases God. "Without faith it is impossible to please him" (Heb. 11:6). Higher levels of glory always mean greater measures of faith. This is the way God has generally chosen for His people to grow.

> We rejoice in hope of the glory of God. Not only
> that, but we rejoice in our sufferings, knowing that
> suffering produces endurance, and endurance pro-
> duces character, and character produces hope, and
> hope does not put us to shame, because God's love
> has been poured into our hearts through the Holy
> Spirit who has been given to us.
>
> —ROMANS 5:2–5

Dignifying the trial is often the next step for us in our walk with the Lord. The trial could be a big one, or it may be a small one. But trials are not going to go away until we are in heaven. So get used to them! And learn to accept them as God's gift. The day will come that you will be able to say that you can hardly tell the difference between a blessing and a trial.

Of course we hope they don't come! That is why we pray the Lord's Prayer, "Lead us not *into* temptation" (Matt. 6:13, emphasis added). Daily we pray that God spares us from trials. But if and when they do come, know it is part of God's sovereign strategy to make us better men and women.

## How to Dignify the Trial

Before I close this chapter, I want to share some practical things you can do to dignify any trial that comes your way.

### 1. Accept the trial when it happens.

Don't show contempt for the very way God has chosen to enable you to have more of Him. Sometimes a person knocks on our doors that we were not expecting. What do you do? You show cordiality and respect. A trial is God knocking on your door at a most inconvenient time. Treat the unexpected with the dignity you would show if a celebrity came to see you.

### 2. Don't panic.

Your first reaction to sudden testing, such as losing your keys or being faced with a horrible ordeal, is to panic. Knowing God is in control of your test can help you at this moment. I will never forget a man from an African nation who came into the vestry to thank me for a word in my public prayer that morning. I had said, "You are a God who does not panic." It was just what he needed. He explained that he was running for office—to be president of his country.

### 3. Know that God has a purpose in it.

This is wonderful news. No trial in your life is without purpose; God's gift to you is for your good. You may not discover in a day or two *why* God gives the trial. But you can be sure that when God is at the bottom of something, it has a definite purpose for *you*. It is what you need at the time. There are no accidents with God. They seem to be accidents to you and me but not to Him.

### 4. Remember that the trial will end.

Never forget that all trials have a built-in time span. They are designed to refine your gold. "The flames will not hurt you; I only design your dross to consume and your gold to refine" (anonymous).[4] God will not let the trial last one day longer than you need. He who sees the end from the beginning has already determined how long the trial will last. Remember, when it's over, it's over. You then reflect.

### 5. Remember that the trial—however brief or long—is an exam.

You pass or fail. I will never forget a severe, sudden ordeal Louise and I experienced during our first year in London. Scotland Yard had just notified us that our driving licenses were not valid and we must not drive. I

134

was warned, "Do not let the wheel roll one inch from your driveway." That came at 3:25 p.m.—literally as Louise was walking out the door to pick up our children from school. I stopped her and explained the phone call. I said to her: "God is giving us an opportunity to dignify this trial. I have failed many times in the past. I want to get an A+ from God on this trial! I don't know what we are going to do, but I refuse to panic or complain." She agreed. Things worked out; a friend went to get the children. We then had to take driving tests to qualify for a license. Those were difficult days but also a turning point in our growth.

### 6. Don't complain.

As I said in an earlier chapter, if we realized how much God hates grumbling and complaining, I think we'd stop it. The quote "Never complain, never explain, never apologize" has been attributed to many sources, including the British Special Air Service and the British Secret Service. It's likely associated with them because it is part of the British "stiff upper lip" syndrome. I don't agree with the phrase "never apologize"—something we all need to do from time to time. But learning not to complain, murmur, or grumble is tantamount to dignifying the trials God has designed for us.

### 7. Remember that dignifying the trial shows you genuinely want more of God.

Keep that passage in mind: "Those who feared the LORD spoke with one another. The LORD paid attention and heard them, and a book of remembrance was written before him of those who feared the LORD and esteemed his name" (Mal. 3:16).

When you are in the middle of a trial, remember that the Lord is watching you! Ask yourself, "Do I want more of God or not? Now is my chance to prove whether I really want more of God."

I now address the reader who is at this very moment in the greatest trial of his life. Is that you? I would urge you to consider these words: the trial will end. When it's over, it's over—and you will wish you had honored God during this ordeal. If you do honor Him, you will never be sorry. Not only that; when the trial ends and you have the satisfaction of having dignified it, the peace and sense of God's approval are so sweet. I guarantee it.

Do you really want more of God?

# Chapter 8

# TOTAL FORGIVENESS

*...forgiving one another, as God in Christ forgave you.*
—EPHESIANS 4:32

THE GREATEST TRIAL Louise and I ever had was not regarding sickness, health problems, financial problems, family difficulties, or tension in our marriage. It had to do with a sense of betrayal. The most significant trial of our lives was while we were at Westminster Chapel. What happened gutted us and left us with the bleakest future we ever imagined. And it was something we could not talk about with anyone.

But there was an exception—Josef Tson of Romania. Some of my readers know the story. I told Josef pretty much everything that happened and what "they" had done, knowing he would not tell a single soul. I think I expected—and hoped—he would put his arm around me and say, "R. T., you should be angry." But no. He merely looked at me and said, "R. T., you must *totally forgive them. Until you totally forgive them*, you will be in chains. Release them, and you will be released."

That is the greatest word anybody ever said to me. "Faithful are the wounds of a friend" (Prov. 27:6, KJV). It changed my life forever. It wasn't easy to take. I protested and said, "Josef, I just remembered that there is one more thing I didn't tell you"—at which point he interrupted me: "R. T., you must *totally forgeeve* them" is the way I remember it sounded with his Romanian accent. "Release them, and you will be released" are the words I could not dismiss.

I can honestly say that I did it. I forgave all those involved. I really did. But after a while I would find myself agitated and hurt way down deep inside, feeling anger because "nobody would know." That's the thing about being hurt. You want everybody to know. When this well of bitterness would erupt, I had to forgive all over again— that is, on the inside.

In most—if not all—cases you should *never* tell the people who don't ask for it, "I forgive you." No. It will be counterproductive every time. You can make things a thousand times worse. They might see you as pointing the finger at them. They will say, "What do you think I have done wrong?" Like it or not, nearly all people we ever need to forgive sincerely and honestly don't believe they have done anything wrong. It will almost always be a case that (1) they don't know we are deeply hurt, or (2) they cannot understand why we are hurt. For example, you could put the people I had to forgive under a lie detector, and they would pass with flying colors, truly believing they did *nothing wrong whatever*. I can safely assume this is what you face too; the people you have to forgive feel utterly innocent of any wrongdoing. That's what hurts and why it is even harder to forgive them.

When they say, "I'm so very sorry, so ashamed of myself," it is easier to forgive. It takes minimal grace to forgive people who are sorry for what they did.

The only time you should say, "I forgive you," is when someone is *asking* for it. That's different. When someone says, "Please forgive me for what I did," then—and only then—should you say, "I forgive you."

Almost certainly the hardest thing you will ever have to do—ever—is let those off the hook who don't know that they hurt you deeply, that they damaged you. It is hard to let those off the hook who wanted to sink you, ruin your reputation, and—if they could—destroy you. It is extremely hard when they don't know what they did. It is even harder when they know what they did and are not sorry.

Either way, we have no choice. I'm sorry, but the only way forward—if you want more of God—is to forgive them. Totally.

## THREE CLARIFICATIONS

Three clarifications are needed here. First, total forgiveness is an act of the will. It is what you choose to do. Don't wait for God to knock you down. He won't. Total forgiveness comes from the inner persuasion of the Holy Spirit that this is something you must do. You know in your heart you should do it. But you must choose to do it. *And do it.* Or you will never do it. After all, it goes against nature and is almost certainly the hardest thing you and I are ever required to do.

Second, total forgiveness is not approving of what they did. Some say, "If I forgive them, they will take it as approval of their wrong." No. When Jesus forgave the woman caught in the act of adultery, He told her that (1) He did not condemn her and (2) she should leave her life of sin (John 8:11). He clearly did not approve of what she did, and this woman would have known this completely.

Third, some mistake total forgiveness for living in denial. I think there is a danger of thinking you have forgiven when it is rather a case that you are in denial. That means you repress or deny what your enemy did, consciously or unconsciously. Sometimes the horror of what the trespasser has done moves in on people's emotions to the degree they can't imagine how bad it really was—and pretend it wasn't so bad.

You don't truly forgive when you live in denial. You forgive when you clearly see what someone did and consciously admit to yourself, "What he did was horrible, unjust, and unthinkably evil." And you *then forgive.* With your eyes wide open. It is not total forgiveness when you live in denial. It is not total forgiveness until you come to terms with how horrible the deed was but *still* let the person completely off the hook. Total forgiveness means you keep no record of wrongs (1 Cor. 13:5). But you clearly *see* the wrongs you choose not to keep a record of.

It takes a lot of grace. But this is when you cross over into the supernatural. You are doing what nature cannot explain—namely, abandoning vengeance and leaving everything to God.

We've all got a story to tell. Many readers of these lines have been hurt far, far worse than I have. Perhaps you were raped. Perhaps you were abused as a child—either by a relative, an authority figure, a leader, or a spiritual leader. Chances are the person will deny that he or she ever did anything wrong to you. Perhaps your spouse was unfaithful to you—and he or she blames you for it. Perhaps your best friend let you down or even betrayed you. Perhaps you were falsely accused of wrongdoing, and everybody believes the lie. Perhaps you were the victim of racial prejudice. Perhaps some people hate you because of the color of your skin. Or because of the neighborhood where you live. They hate you because they have a different set of beliefs than yours. They hate you because they are jealous of you. They hate you because of your looks. They hate you because of your wealth. Or your success. Or your ability. Or your connections. Or your background. Or your education. Or your job. Perhaps you were falsely imprisoned. Perhaps someone robbed you—and you lost a lot of money. Perhaps someone robbed you of a good reputation. Perhaps you were promised a position, but it went to another—even a friend. Or an enemy. Perhaps someone stole money from you. Perhaps someone flirted with your spouse. Maybe it was your best friend. Perhaps someone put stuff on the internet about you that is completely untrue. Perhaps someone stopped speaking to you for no good reason. Perhaps someone kept you from getting the interview you wanted. Perhaps someone murdered your closest friend or relative. I could go on and on.

Here is what I believe: the greater the suffering, the greater the anointing. Your suffering is not for nothing— that is, *if*—and this is a huge *if*—you will *totally* forgive your offender. This means you let him or her off the hook, completely. It means you pray for the person—that God will truly *bless* him or her and not merely "deal" with that person! (When you ask God to deal with that person, you are possibly hoping God will kill him or her! Or at least make the person suffer.)

I also fear it is true that the greater the anointing, the greater the suffering. Perhaps not always. But many highly anointed people suffer a lot. Those in the Bible who had a great anointing on them were among those who suffered much—Abraham, Isaac, Jacob, Joseph, Moses, Samuel, Isaiah, Jeremiah, and others. Great anointing is often crowned with suffering lest we begin to take ourselves too seriously. If you have a special position or role to play in God's kingdom, chances are you will experience a greater dose of suffering than those around you who have less responsibility. That suffering could be physical—such as an incurable cough, illness, or disease—or it could be suffering from persecution for your faith.

## THE BOTTOM LINE

Here's the issue: Do you want more of God? Do you? Do you want more of God no matter the cost? What if it costs you all you have (Prov. 4:7)? Do you still want more of God?

Have you ever said something like this: "I will never forgive him for what he did"? Have you threatened someone with these words, "I won't forget that" (meaning that you won't let what she said go unpunished)? John F. Kennedy was famous for saying, "Forgive your enemies, but never forget their names."[1]

I don't mean to be unfair, but it is just possible that someone reading these lines will come to the crossroads with this choice: Do I get even and wait for vengeance, or do I want more of God?

Are you willing to kiss vengeance goodbye? Do you realize that vengeance is God's prerogative? "Vengeance is mine" (Rom. 12:19; Deut. 32:35). "Yes, I know," you might say, "but He is so slow." I can assure you, God cares about your feelings. He cares about the person who has suffered, been falsely accused, been raped, been marginalized by racial prejudice—plus a thousand more things I could mention. But let *Him* handle it! Here is the best advice you will get:

> Do not repay evil for evil or reviling for reviling, but
> on the contrary, bless, for to this you were called,
> that you may obtain a blessing. For "Whoever

> desires to love life and see good days, let him keep
> his tongue from evil and his lips from speaking
> deceit; let him turn away from evil and do good; let
> him seek peace and pursue it. For the eyes of the
> Lord are on the righteous, and his ears are open to
> their prayer. But the face of the Lord is against those
> who do evil." Now who is there to harm you if you
> are zealous for what is good? But even if you should
> suffer for righteousness' sake, you will be blessed.
>
> —1 Peter 3:9–14

I can promise you something categorically: if vengeance
upon your enemy is what is best for you, that will certainly come down the road at some stage. But it is equally
true that while you wait for revenge, you can get to know
God's ways—and, not unlikely, discovering His ways will
give you more satisfaction than anything else. I am not
saying God will not bring vengeance upon those who
have maligned you; He may do just that—but only if that
is what is best for you! "No good thing does he withhold"
from you if you want more of Him than anything else (Ps.
84:11). He may give you the double joy of having more of
Him *plus* bringing vengeance upon your enemy. Yes, He
might do that. But it is also possible that when you experience the joy of more of Him, your desire for revenge will
evaporate like water before the hot sun.

Do you want vindication over something in the past?
Are you willing to abandon vindication in order to have
more of God? Vindication and vengeance are similar. God
is responsible for both. It is what He does. Vengeance
comes when your enemy is punished; vindication is when

your name is cleared. Both have to do with your pride and self-esteem. And God takes the responsibility of doing both. By the way, He does not want your help. As a matter of fact, if you try to help Him, He may well back off your case entirely and let you handle it (for you to see how much worse it gets when you take matters into your own hands).

Here's a good rule: don't rob God of the privilege of doing what He does best. Don't take from Him the joy of what He loves to do. And don't try to figure out how He will do it. I can only say He is brilliant at this. You with your ingenuity could never—ever—come close to the way God will do it—on this condition: you let Him handle it. If you are curious as to how brilliant He is when it comes to vindication and vengeance, read the Book of Esther and see how God vindicated Mordecai and brought vengeance on Mordecai's enemy (2:21–7:10).

What do you suppose would give you more strength? Or energy? Or fun? Or pleasure? Or joy? Would you be willing for the joy of the Lord to be your strength (Neh. 8:10)? Do you realize that the joy of the Holy Spirit is not only a discipline—by walking in the Spirit—but that the person of the Holy Spirit Himself is full of joy? Yes, the third person of the Trinity—the Holy Spirit—is a joyful person! God the Father is a joyful person (Ps. 16:11). Jesus Christ is full of joy (John 15:11).

In other words, getting more of God will mean more joy! It will also correct your blood pressure and give you good health and more years. More than that, God will use you in a way you never dreamed possible. *Don't deprive God of doing this. He is good at it.*

Getting vengeance on those who have hurt you is the most natural desire on earth. You don't need to learn how to increase your desire for revenge—or vindication—by taking a class at a university! Some things don't need to be taught, and when it comes to our ego, no further learning is needed. As the desire for sexual fulfillment is a natural gift by creation, so too is the desire for significance. The craving for vindication or vengeance flows from a natural appetite that pertains to our self-esteem.

Therefore, the willingness to forgive totally and abandon vengeance or vindication is supernatural. Supernatural means that it is above nature. It is something that God gives. When you totally forgive, you have crossed over into the supernatural.

Would you like to cross over into the realm of the supernatural? Then let your offenders off the hook. Pray for them—that they will be blessed.

You may ask, "Aren't there other ways to get more of God?" Perhaps. We saw in the previous chapter that dignifying the trial is one example; do that, and it will lead you to more of God. This entire book is about how to get more of God. However, if I've got it right, we cannot be selective with the options that lead us to receive more of God. If we truly want more of God, we will take with both hands *anything* that moves us closer to getting more of Him.

Or are you into "Brylcreem religion"? Forgive me for this silly comparison; I refer to an old product that people used for their hair. Its slogan was "A little dab will do you." Do you want merely a "little dab" of the Holy Spirit? I'm afraid too many are into "Brylcreem religion." Don't be one of them. Don't settle for folk religion.

## HOW DO WE KNOW WE HAVE TOTALLY FORGIVEN?

The question follows: How do we know we have totally forgiven? Assuming that you, the reader, want more of God—knowing that total forgiveness is demonstrating you want more of God—we need to know if we *have indeed totally forgiven those who have hurt us in any way.* The question therefore is, If I can show in the remainder of this chapter that you have *not* totally forgiven those who have hurt you, would you then be willing to do so? This chapter will bring us to the crossroads—decision time. You will have an opportunity to make the next move forward in showing you want more of God.

So how can we be sure we want more of God? Paul said we should forgive as God in Christ has forgiven us (Eph. 4:32; Col. 3:13). To what extent, then, has God forgiven us?

### 1. We will tell no one what "they" did to us.

God will not tell others what sins you and I have committed. He has the "goods" on all of us. But God has promised to forget them: "He will again have compassion on us; he will tread our iniquities underfoot. You will cast all our sins into the depths of the sea" (Mic. 7:19).

I don't know about you, of course, but I will tell you candidly, God has enough on me to destroy me and bury me so that no one would want to see me or hear me speak again. But guess what? *You will never know.* "As far as the east is from the west, so far does he remove our transgressions from us" (Ps. 103:12).

And yet I must add, although God has chosen to "forget" my sins, it is not as though He lost His memory! Of course He knows full well of what He has forgiven me! Proof of this is what Jesus taught. Having told us to forgive "not...seven times, but seventy-seven times" (Matt. 18:22; some versions say "up to seventy times seven"), He gave the famous parable of the unmerciful servant:

> Therefore the kingdom of heaven is like a certain king who wanted to settle accounts with his servants. When he began to settle the accounts, one was brought to him who owed him ten thousand talents. But since he was not able to pay, his master ordered that he be sold with his wife, their children, and all that he had, and payment to be made. So the servant fell on his knees, pleading with him, saying, "Master, have patience with me, and I will pay you everything." Then the master of that servant was moved with compassion, released him, and forgave him the debt. But that same servant went out and found one of his fellow servants who owed him a hundred denarii. He laid hands on him and took him by the throat, saying, "Pay me what you owe." So his fellow servant fell down at his feet and entreated him, saying, "Have patience with me, and I will pay you everything." But he would not and went and threw him in prison until he should pay the debt. So when his fellow servants saw what took place, they were very sorry and went and told their

master all that had taken place. Then his master, after he had summoned him, said to him, "O you wicked servant! I forgave you all that debt because you pleaded with me. Should you not also have had compassion on your fellow servant, even as I had pity on you?" His master was angry and delivered him to the jailers until he should pay all his debt. So also My heavenly Father will do to each of you, if from your heart you do not forgive your brother for his trespasses.

—MATTHEW 18:23–35, MEV

The master in this parable clearly knew what he had forgiven but then took it back when forgiveness was not passed on! When God has forgiven us, He expects us to pass it on. When you have wronged me, hurt me, or betrayed me, and I tell others what you did, I have broken the assumption that I would forgive as I have been forgiven. God does not like it one bit. So when I tell the world the injustice you have done to me when He knows full well that He has forgiven me, He is angry and will deal with me without a doubt. This does not mean I lose my salvation, but it *does* mean I forfeit getting more of God. He expects me to forgive others in proportion to the way He has forgiven me.

If I want more of God, I will not pass on to anyone how you have wronged me. I can tell the Lord what you have done. That's fine. After all, God wants us to pour out our complaint to Him! He has big shoulders: "With my voice I cry out to the LORD; with my voice I plead for mercy to the LORD. I pour out my complaint before him; I tell my trouble before him" (Ps. 142:1–2).

God likes it when He is the *only* one you tell. This way you are confiding in Him. You honor Him by telling Him and only Him what people did to you. But when you tell others and also tell the Lord, He is merely one more in a number who know this person has hurt you. This makes me think of the old spiritual that came out of the Deep South in the nineteenth century, reflecting the pain of the slaves working in the cotton fields:

> Nobody knows the trouble I've seen;
> Nobody knows but Jesus.
>
> —ANONYMOUS

Joseph beautifully illustrates this (as I write in my books *God Meant It for Good* and *Total Forgiveness*). He knew exactly what his brothers had done to him—that they had planned to kill him but at the last minute sold him to the Ishmaelites (Gen. 37:19–28). Knowing as he did—because of dreams God gave him—that his brothers would one day bow down to him, I suppose he thought he would one day look at those brothers and say, "Gotcha!" and make them pay. He could have thrown the book at them since he was now the prime minister of Egypt. But by the time the dreams were fulfilled, Joseph was a changed man—a new man, a broken man. Instead of punishing them, he said, "Make everyone go out from me" (Gen. 45:1). Joseph made sure that there was no one in the room but himself and his eleven brothers.

But why? It was because he wanted to ensure nobody

in Egypt would ever—ever—find out what his eleven brothers would have done to him. Joseph knew that he was a hero in Egypt. He wanted his brothers to bring his father, Jacob, from Canaan and live in Egypt. He wanted all of Egypt to admire his brothers. He knew that if the word leaked out, every Egyptian to a man would hate his brothers. He wanted to make sure that *no one* in Egypt would ever find out about the cruelty of his brothers. So behind closed doors Joseph revealed his identity to his brothers and demonstrated total forgiveness to them.

He was a type of Christ—someone in the Old Testament who makes you think of Jesus before Jesus came along. Joseph demonstrated true godliness, showing mercy as God shows mercy (Luke 6:36). As God will not tell the world of your sins or mine, so Joseph was demonstrating that nobody in Egypt would ever suspect that his brothers had been unkind to him.

Is it not true that when people malign us, we get right on the phone to tell people what "they" did? Why? It is because we cannot bear the thought of anybody admiring them anymore! We cannot stand thinking that the world admires people who have been so malicious. Also, we want to punish our enemies by telling on them! So we tell what they did.

This we must never do.

But there are two exceptions. First, you need to share with *one other person* the evil that was done to you. For therapeutic reasons, you need to tell a friend—someone who will never repeat it to anyone else. Tell a close friend, pastor, vicar, or counselor. You can tell one. But not two.

Or two hundred! You can tell one other person and should do this.

Second, a *crime must be reported*. A lady came into the vestry of Westminster Chapel to say, "They have found my rapist and now want me to testify in a court of law."

I replied, "You must."

"But oh, Dr. Kendall, you taught me to forgive, and I have forgiven him."

I said to her, "Well done. I believe you. I'm so proud of you for that. But this is a crime. You have forgiven him. It is not personal. All you have to do is answer their questions." She did.

There may be a third exception in some cases—sharing a testimony with someone who could be helped by what you have been through. Caution: be careful not to make your offender look bad, and if possible conceal his identity. As long as you are not wishing to make a person look bad but only to share what you have been through for God's glory, this might be helpful to some.

Outside of these three exceptions you should stick to the rule of telling no one, because outside of these three reasons what is the real reason we tell? To get even. To punish. "But perfect love casts out fear. For fear has to do with punishment" (1 John 4:18). Perfect love removes the need to punish, to get even.

When you and I truly want more of God, we will not try to get even with those who have been unjust; we will let God handle the whole matter. It is His problem. He wants the problem. He welcomes the problem. But when we tell what "they" did, we have robbed Him of what He longs to do for us. Don't deprive our heavenly Father of demonstrating His expertise.

## 2. We won't let them be afraid of us.

When Joseph without his interpreter spoke to his brothers in their language, "I am Joseph!" they were scared to death. They were "dismayed" being in Joseph's presence (Gen. 45:3).

It was an emotional moment for Joseph. "He wept aloud, so that the Egyptians heard it, and the household of Pharaoh heard it" (v. 2). Whereas this might be explained by an ancient Middle Eastern culture—as when Jacob wept "aloud" when he first saw Rachel (Gen. 29:11)—there is perhaps more going on here. When one hopes to say "Gotcha!" and instead suddenly lets them off the hook, it could be simultaneous pain and relief. It hurts to forgive. You are giving up a long-awaited moment to see vengeance. You kiss that goodbye. It can be incalculably painful, but it also emancipates. When I invite people to forgive those who hurt them and they respond positively, there can be a lot of tears.

On the other hand, I have watched those who equally forgive and show no emotion. What matters is commitment—a resolve, an act of the will that you never revoke.

Joseph's loud weeping did not indicate that he forgave them; it was his saying to them, "Come near to me" (Gen. 45:4). He knew they were nervous and afraid. The irony is, it was probably what he always wanted—to see them afraid of him! But now he had it on a silver platter—and

153

rejected it: "Come near to me." He only wanted to love on them. "Perfect love casts out fear" (1 John 4:18).

Total forgiveness is when you put your enemy at ease. Instead of wanting the person to be on edge and anxious, you treat him or her with kindness and dignity. That is what Joseph was doing. He did not want them to be afraid of him.

### 3. We refuse to make them feel guilty.

Joseph knew his brothers felt horrible about how they treated him some twenty years earlier, so he said, "Do not be distressed or angry with yourselves because you sold me here" (Gen. 45:5). He tried to ease their pain by assuring them that God was behind it. "God sent me before you."

Be honest for a moment. Have you said to someone, "I forgive you," but you hope the person still feels bad about it? If so, you are still trying to stick the knife into him, to make him squirm. I'm afraid that will not do if you want more of God.

It bears repeating: It takes minimal grace to forgive when your enemies have repented and are sorry. But it takes a *lot* of grace to forgive them when (a) they are not sorry or (b) they don't know that you are hurt or, even more so, (c) they know what they did but don't feel they did anything wrong!

Here is a challenge for you: *forgive them now*—when they don't think they have done anything wrong! Forgive them when they are not sorry! Forgive them when they don't even have a clue that you are hurt. Jesus prayed for those who nailed Him to the cross, "Father, forgive them, for they know not what they do" (Luke 23:34). This is a golden opportunity for you to be like Jesus. Don't blow away this chance to demonstrate Christlike graciousness. If they should ever come around and be sorry, and then you forgive them, your reward—if any—will be minimal. But when you forgive them when they have no sense of shame, "your reward will be great" (Luke 6:35).

Don't be surprised if those you have to forgive are close friends or relatives or those who dwell among the "godly." Oh dear, "godly" people can be so, dare I say it, horrible.

> Living with the saints above, oh that will be glory;
> Living with the saints below, well, that's another
>   story.
> —ANONYMOUS

### 4. You let them save face.

Saving face is (I think) originally an Eastern expression. It means to let the other people avoid humiliation, embarrassment. You protect their fragile egos. You cover for them. Dale Carnegie, who wrote *How to Win Friends and Influence People*, reckons you win a friend for life when you let him or her save face.

How did Joseph let them save face? "It was not you who sent me here, but God" (Gen. 45:8). What he said comes to this: All has gone according to plan. God told our great-grandfather Abraham that his seed would be coming out of Egypt. Someone had to get here first. God simply said, "Joseph, you go first." It was Joseph's way of saying, "I would have done what you did had I been one of you!"

I don't think these eleven brothers could believe their

luck! They must have been trying to absorb what Joseph conveyed to them: "Joseph says we didn't do it. God did it." They were trying to grasp what was going on: "The very man we were going to kill is now saying, 'God did it.'" That's it, says Joseph: "For the famine has been in the land these two years, and there are yet five years in which there will be neither plowing nor harvest. And God sent me before you to preserve for you a remnant on earth, and to keep alive for you many survivors. So it was not you who sent me here, but God" (Gen. 45:6–8).

Amazing. Total deliverance is refusing to rub their noses in it but letting them save face, giving them a way out so they can live with themselves.

### 5. You protect them from their darkest secret.

Chances are, you know something about someone that—if known by others—could destroy him. And what if you have the "goods" on your enemy? Will you use this to destroy him?

What was the dark secret of Joseph's brothers? They had taken a colorful coat that Jacob made for Joseph and dipped it in blood. They sent the richly ornamented robe to Jacob to see if he recognized it. He did (Gen. 37:31–35). You can be sure that these brothers would rather die than have to tell their father the truth of what happened.

This is so moving; Joseph won't let them tell the old man! He tells them what to say when they are to return to Jacob. He writes the script for them. He won't allow them to tell the truth of what they did. This is more than saving face; it is protecting them from their deepest secret.

We all have skeletons in the closet. God does not want to yank the skeleton out of the closet and embarrass us. No. He protects us from our deepest, darkest secret.

Total forgiveness is this.

## 5. Maintaining total forgiveness is a life sentence.

Forgive is something you will have to do every day for the rest of your life. It is like a physician's prescription, a tablet you have to take daily for the rest of your life. It's a life sentence.

Joseph demonstrated this when, seventeen years later, Jacob died. His brothers panicked. They came running to Joseph with a plea—thinking this was necessary to save their lives. They believed Joseph was waiting for their father to die so he could then get vengeance on them. We don't know whether they had ever told their father the whole truth or whether Jacob had figured it out on his own. But fearing Joseph would pay them back, they made up a story.

> Your father gave this command before he died: "Say to Joseph, 'Please forgive the transgression of your brothers and their sin, because they did evil to you.'" And now, please forgive the transgression of the servants of the God of your father.
>
> —GENESIS 50:16–17

Joseph wept. His brothers came and threw themselves down before him. "We are your slaves," they said. What follows shows that Joseph *still* forgave them—after all those years. He assured them, "Do not fear, for am I in the place of God? As for you, you meant evil against me, but God meant it for good" (Gen. 50:19–20). Joseph was not remotely thinking of bringing all this up! The truth is, he really had forgiven them!

Total forgiveness is a life sentence. You have to do it today. You have to do it again tomorrow.

You may say, "I did it once—that's enough." I reply, "You have a flawed doctrine of sanctification." "The heart is deceitful above all things, and desperately sick" (Jer. 17:9). For this reason you have to practice godliness every day by forgiving every day—as long as you live. As a matter of fact, this could be the *key* to your wanting more of God— that you keep on forgiving, over and over. I would even say this is the stage where the anointing kicks in! When you show that your resolve to forgive is genuine, you prove it by continuing to forgive.

### 7. You bless them.

"'So do not fear,'" said Joseph; "'I will provide for you and your little ones.' Thus he comforted them and spoke kindly to them" (Gen. 50:21). When you bless your enemy, you have come a long way in demonstrating that you want more of God. There are at least two ways you might bless them. First, you provide for them. You look after them. You don't look back. The very opposite of getting even is blessing them.

Second, you pray for them. Jesus said,

> Love your enemies and pray for those who perse-
> cute you, so that you may be sons of your Father
> who is in heaven. For he makes his sun rise on the

evil and on the good, and sends rain on the just and on the unjust. For if you love those who love you, what reward do you have?

—Matthew 5:44–46

Love your enemies, do good to those who hate you, bless those who curse you, pray for those who abuse you....If you love those who love you, what benefit is that to you?...Even sinners do the same....But love your enemies, and do good, and lend, expecting nothing in return, and your reward will be great, and you will be sons of the Most High, for he is kind to the ungrateful and the evil. Be merciful, even as your Father is merciful.

—Luke 6:27–28, 32–33, 35–36

If you can reach the place where you pray for your enemies and mean what you say, literally asking God to bless them, you are pretty much *there*. That is, you are truly beginning to show you want more of God. I would testify that my greatest sense of anointing came after I started genuinely praying for those who hurt not only me but our children. I found it easier to forgive those who have maligned me than those who have hurt our two children. As every parent knows, when your children hurt, that is the worst pain of all.

Remember, the greater the suffering, the greater the anointing. When you can sincerely pray for those who have hurt you and your loved ones, you get God's attention.

## DECISION TIME

I promised in this chapter to give you an opportunity to forgive. The time has come. I will ask you to make a covenant with God. Caution: this is serious business. Don't do it unless you know what you are doing. You are being watched by the angels and by the Father, Son, and Holy Spirit. In the Old Testament ratifying a covenant required the shedding of blood. That is how serious it was. It is *still* that serious. This is because we are under a covenant made two thousand years ago through the shed blood of Jesus. This is because you are about to make a vow to God. It is better not to make a vow than to make a vow and not keep it.

> When you vow a vow to God, do not delay paying
> it, for he has no pleasure in fools. Pay what you vow.
> It is better that you should not vow than that you
> should vow and not pay.
>
> —ECCLESIASTES 5:4–5

That said, this is something you should do, or you will never cross over the line you seriously need to cross over. Are you ready? If so, pray this prayer:

> *Lord Jesus, I am sorry for my sins. I'm sorry for*
> *my bitterness. I am sorry for my grudge. I am*
> *sorry for my unforgiveness. Wash my sins away*
> *by Your blood. Thank You for dying for me*
> *on the cross for my sins. I welcome Your Holy*
> *Spirit to come into my heart in ever-increasing*
> *measure. I ask You not only to forgive me but*

*to forgive* [fill in their name or names]. *I ask
You to bless them. I ask You to set them free.
I set them free. I set them free. I set them free.
Thank You for Your patience with me. Amen.*

One further caution: when you mess up—and you will—
do not say, "Oh well, I broke my covenant, so I might as
well go back to business as usual." No. That's what the
devil wants you to do. When you err—such as pointing
the finger or telling what they did, *confess it immediately.*
Keep a short account with God. Never forget good old
1 John 1:9: "If we confess our sins, he is faithful and just to
forgive us our sins and to cleanse us from all unrighteous-
ness." Then keep going forward. And remember that total
forgiveness is a life sentence.

# Chapter 9

## PERSONAL DISCIPLINE

*My people are destroyed from lack of knowledge.*
—HOSEA 4:6

ONE OF THE things that has shocked me most in my old age has been my increased awareness of how little today's Christians know their Bibles. There was a day in my lifetime when a typical layman knew his Bible virtually as well as the minister. But those days seem to be over. Alas, even many ministers do not know their Bibles, only consulting them when they need a sermon. The president of my old college—Trevecca Nazarene College (now University) in Nashville, Tennessee—observed that "R. T. came to Trevecca with more knowledge of the Bible than most people leave it with." Now, before you think I am bragging on myself, let me state quickly this is not the case; it is bragging about my parents and my old pastors in Ashland, Kentucky. When I went to Trevecca, I had not intended to study for the ministry. I wanted to be a criminal lawyer for some reason. My point here is, I had been taught to spend time in prayer and Bible reading by my pastors and my parents. I did not know in those days that this was unusual.

I am very worried about the state of the church in America and Britain. England has been my second home for approximately thirty-five years, over half of my adult life. I am deeply indebted to Britain. England has given me my preaching, pastoral, writing, and even television ministry. My debt to the British is incalculable. From my research degree at Oxford to Westminster Chapel to Spring Harvest to Kensington Temple, I would have no ministry apart from Britain.

The spiritual life of Britain was not all that high even when we first arrived at Oxford in 1973. But it has waned to an alarming degree since then. I have watched Muslims increase as Christians decrease in number. I think this is largely traceable to an absence of the fear of God in the church in Britain. This in turn is traceable to the spiritual leadership—whether in Anglican or "free churches."

In America the situation is, if anything, worse. The English Puritans who came to our shores in the seventeenth century gave America its soul. But America has since lost its soul. According to Franklin Graham, "America has changed and it's not coming back unless the church takes a stand."[1] This, in my view, is largely traceable to the spiritual leadership of America, which has allowed Bible-denying liberalism to creep in and destroy the church. My only hope is that there will be a great awakening on both sides of the Atlantic—before the second coming—that will turn things around.

What can we do in the meantime? Seek to get more of God—not more *from* God or more *about* God, but more *of* God.

In this penultimate chapter I want to stress two things: personal prayer and Bible reading. That may seem crass and simplistic. But this is my conviction. These two disciplines must character *all Christians*—whether laymen or those in ministry: ministers, pastors, vicars, bishops, priests, evangelists, and teachers.

## THREE THINGS

"My people are destroyed for lack of knowledge," says Hosea 4:6. I would say knowledge of three things: God's Word, His ways, and His wisdom.

### 1. Personal reading of the Scriptures

Do you read your Bible? How often? How well do you know your Bible? In Martin Luther's day people didn't have Bibles, and therefore, they couldn't read them. Today we have Bibles but don't read them. The result is that we are virtually as ignorant of the Scriptures as Christians were in Luther's day. When Luther translated the Bible into German, people read their Bibles with eagerness.

Preaching became popular. Knowledge of the Scriptures flourished. It turned the world upside down.

Our greatest sin today is ingratitude. We are like the pharaoh who knew not Joseph (Exod. 1:8). Joseph gave Egypt a reason to live; he transformed the nation. He was a hero for an entire generation. But the pharaoh who was so grateful to Joseph died. The next pharaoh did not feel a debt to Joseph and saw the Israelites growing. Instead of being grateful, he felt threatened. He turned on the Israelites and made them suffer.

Whether in America or Britain, those in the present generation shows no thanks or appreciation to their Christian heritage. The thought annoys them. They resist any effort to show gratitude. Take the BBC. Embedded in the concrete floor of Broadcasting House is this verse:

> Whatsoever things are true, whatsoever things are honest, whatsoever things are just, whatsoever things are pure, whatsoever things are lovely, whatsoever things are of good report; if there be any virtue, and if there be any praise, think on these things.
>
> —PHILIPPIANS 4:8, KJV

This verse is an embarrassment to the BBC today. It is disdained and resented. And yet this thinking is what launched the BBC in 1922, nearly one hundred years ago. The purpose of choosing Philippians 4:8 was that the BBC would be the vehicle of what is honest, just, pure, lovely, and so on. There was a sense of the fear of God behind choosing this verse. But that was then.

Consider universities such as Harvard, Yale, and Princeton. These schools were founded upon God-fearing principles—by the Puritans who came to America. But there is an utter absence of staunch biblical beliefs in these universities today. The Bible is laughed at, is torn to shreds, and is the last book most people would seriously consider when forming theology today. This was the case at Southern Baptist Theological Seminary when I was there from 1971 to 1973. My New Testament professors did not believe in the resurrection of Jesus Christ from the dead but rather championed the Rudolf Bultmanns of this world. Nearly all the professors in those days were keener on being seen as erudite scholars than as Evangelicals who were not respected by the German theologians. What Harvard or Tübingen thought meant more to them than what ordinary Christians thought. I vividly recall a graduate student saying to me in 1973, "I am leaving Southern Seminary with nothing to do. I came to this place believing in the Bible. But they have shown me that it is a faulty document, and I don't know where I will go."

That has changed in some seminaries since then, for which we thank God.

Why read the Bible? First, it is the infallible Word of God. You can believe what it says; you can embrace what it says. The Holy Spirit wrote it through human instruments. God has preserved it across the centuries. And if you want to know why God has blessed Billy Graham, the Gideons, Arthur Blessitt, and others, it is because they uphold *the Bible* unashamedly. "The Bible says" was Billy

Graham's most frequent phrase and that for which he became famous.

Why read the Bible? Second, you believe it will preserve you from disaster and failure. Through the unwavering belief in the Scriptures, you will have principles embedded in you that will hold you in the storms of life. It is exactly what Jesus promised:

> Everyone then who hears these words of mine and does them will be like a wise man who built his house on the rock. And the rain fell, and the floods came, and the winds blew and beat on that house, but it did not fall, because it had been founded on the rock. And everyone who hears these words of mine and does not do them will be like a foolish man who built his house on the sand. And the rain fell, and the floods came, and the winds blew and beat against that house, and it fell, and great was the fall of it.
> —MATTHEW 7:24–27

Whether you are a layman or church leader, the degree to which you read, believe, and uphold Scripture in your mind, heart, and practice will be the degree to which your heavenly Father will bless you. You will never be sorry—that I can guarantee!

Why read the Bible? Third, the Holy Spirit will remind you of what you have read. You may feel bored and un-inspired at times when you read the Bible. I say read it anyway! Keep on reading. Do not stop. There will be a moment down the road—I promise this—when the Holy

Spirit will remind you of what you read, just as Jesus promised in John 14:26. But if you have not read the Bible, there will be nothing in your head for the Holy Spirit to work with! You will be empty-headed and stay that way. Don't let that happen to you!

I say this with tongue in cheek, but would you like a bit of "secret information"? Would you like a "tip" as to how to get on the "good side" of the Holy Spirit (if you will allow me to put it this way)? I can tell you: get to know His Word. The Holy Spirit wrote it. He is unashamed of what He wrote—Holy Scripture. God has magnified His Word above His name (Ps. 138:2, KJV). Get to know His Word, and the Holy Spirit will honor you to the hilt. What is more, getting on the good side of the Holy Spirit means getting more of Him. Never forget that the Holy Spirit is God! Getting more of the Holy Spirit is the same as getting more of God. The more you know of His greatest product—the Bible—the more you get of God.

## 2. Quiet time in prayer alone with God

My father was not a preacher. He was a layman. He was a rate clerk with the Chesapeake and Ohio Railway. The nearest he came to being a preacher was he taught a Sunday school class that was attended weekly by some forty people. My first memory of him was seeing him on his knees every morning for thirty minutes before he went to work. A couple of years before he died, I asked him, "Dad, why did you pray so much? You spent more time in prayer than most preachers do."

He replied, "Pastor Gene Phillips tried to get every

member to pray for thirty minutes a day, and I did." I don't think he thought it was unusual. I'm sure these thirty minutes included his Bible reading time. He knew his Bible, I can tell you. On his tombstone in Fitzgerald, Georgia, we put these words: "A man of prayer." Oh yes. So true.

I grew up thinking my dad's time alone with God every morning was normal. I now concede that it was unusual, but in any case he passed it on to me. For this reason I can take no credit for the way I read my Bible and prayed as I grew up.

I hope there will be readers—young and old, ministers and laymen—who will want to be like this. Please listen to me! It will save you from much sorrow and regret.

"My people are destroyed for lack of knowledge." You get to know His Word by reading the Bible. You get to know His ways by spending time with him. You show your esteem of another person by how much time you give them. Children spell *love* T-I-M-E. If God assesses your love for Him by how much *time* you give Him, how does this make you feel?

There will be no praying in heaven. When I said this a few years ago at Westminster Chapel, it upset a lovely deaf lady. She said she enjoyed her quiet time so much; the thought that she would not have this in heaven disappointed her. But that is the way it will be. There will be no need to pray in heaven. One hymn writer grasped this when writing the last verse of the hymn "Sweet Hour of Prayer:"

> Sweet hour of prayer, sweet hour of prayer,
> May I thy consolation share,

Till, from Mount Pisgah's lofty height,
I view my home and take my flight:
This robe of flesh I'll drop and rise
To seize the everlasting prize;
And shout, while passing through the air,
"Farewell, farewell, sweet hour of prayer!"[2]
—WILLIAM W. WALFORD (1772–1850)

Time spent alone with God in prayer is not wasted. Apart from being one more example of building your superstructure with gold, silver, and precious gems, what it will do for you on this earth cannot be calculated. I can say this much: it will make all the difference in your anointing, your ability to understand the Bible, and—most of all—getting more of God in your life.

When you stand before God at the judgment seat of Christ, you may have many regrets over the way you spent your time and money, but you will not regret time spent alone with God. You cannot get those hours back. They show to a considerable degree how much God means to you.

Prayer is your source of power. "You will receive power," said Jesus (Acts 1:8). The disciples consequently spent the next ten days in prayer before the Holy Spirit fell on them. Time spent with God plus no one else is one of the best ways to know God's ways. God has "ways." God lamented of ancient Israel, "They have not known my ways" (Heb. 3:10). God wants you to know His ways. He wants you to like His ways! But you will hardly get to know His ways when you don't have time for Him. You can read about His ways in books—including mine. But all my books are no substitute for the time you need to spend alone with God.

As I say in my book *Did You Think to Pray?*, Martin Luther prayed for *two hours* every day. John Wesley prayed for *two hours* every day. The average church leader on both sides of the Atlantic today prays for *four minutes* a day. And you wonder why the church is powerless?

How much do you pray?

### 3. An unfeigned fear of God

This is the way forward if you want God's wisdom. As we will see further, the fear of the Lord is the beginning of understanding, knowledge, and wisdom.

The way forward to wisdom is quite simple. It does not require a university education, good breeding, a high IQ, or being well connected. It is simple: you receive wisdom when you have a true fear of the Lord.

Does this mean being afraid of God? Yes and no. Yes, when you consider that He holds your destiny in His hands, that the wrath of God is coming, and that He is the architect of the idea of hell. I think that is enough to make you afraid of Him. That is what brought hundreds from Jerusalem to hear John the Baptist. The first message of the New Testament is, "Who warned you to flee from the wrath to come?" (Matt. 3:7). When John the Baptist asked that question, the assumption was, "Somebody should have warned you. Who has warned you? Has anyone? If not, they have let you down; they have done you no favor not to warn you."

One of the most forgotten messages of the Bible is that we are saved from the "wrath to come" (1 Thess. 1:10).

God's wrath is the reason for the gospel (Rom. 1:18). As I mentioned earlier, when Jonathan Edwards finished his sermon "Sinners in the Hands of an Angry God" (July 8, 1741), people were scared to death. They held on to pews and tree trunks to keep from sliding into hell, which tells me they were afraid of God.

Here's the thing: We in our generation understandably don't want to be regarded as people who say you should be afraid of God; after all, nowadays that way of thinking is seen as both antiquated and cruel. Many of us consequently rush to give God better "press." We try to stress that the fear of God only means "awe" or "respect." I can truly understand why people do this. But has it worked? Has it brought people back to church? Not at all.

Not only that; it is my opinion that when the midnight cry (Matt. 25:6) comes—the next thing to happen on God's calendar—people will be scared to death. People were scared to death when the Twin Towers fell in New York City on September 11, 2001. But the midnight cry will make even that look like nothing by comparison. The authority of the message itself will do that. In any case when people see Jesus in the clouds with great glory, they will not only weep and cry but "wail" because of Him (Rev. 1:7). This can only mean they are afraid.

That said, of course I accept that God does not want us to be afraid of him sixty seconds a minute, twenty-four hours a day. That would produce neurotics and weird people. I don't want this any more than you do. So no, God does not want us to be afraid of Him twenty-four hours a day—only to remember that He is a jealous God, a

God who hates sin, and a God who will punish sin. What He wants of us is the level of respect for Him that changes our lives; that is what the Book of Proverbs is after:

> The fear of the LORD is the beginning of knowledge;
> fools despise wisdom and instruction.
> —PROVERBS 1:7

> The fear of the LORD is the beginning of wisdom,
> and the knowledge of the Holy One is insight.
> —PROVERBS 9:10

To put it another way, have you noticed how many "in your face" references there are to sexual promiscuity and sexual purity in Proverbs? Read Proverbs 6:20–35, Proverbs 7, and many others. There is an inseparable connection between sexual purity and wisdom. If you indulge in sex outside of heterosexual marriage, you forfeit wisdom, says Proverbs. You cannot have it both ways. If you want wisdom, you will be sexually pure. If you want to be a fool, become sexually promiscuous. Dismiss what I say here, and you will mess up big time and never get over it.

In other words, sexual purity is a sign that you truly fear the Lord—whether it comes from being afraid or respectful. Whatever adjective you use to describe what the fear of the Lord means, avoid sexual promiscuity if you want wisdom.

God's wisdom transcends all other kinds of wisdom— philosophy, Buddhism, psychology, or mathematics. God's wisdom is the presence of His mind. His wisdom may not make you an Einstein or a great mathematician, but you will accomplish more with it than you will ever accomplish without it. Not only that, as John Wesley used to say of the early Methodists: "Our people die well."[3] When you get more of God, you will get more wisdom than you ever dreamed of having. Moreover, as I quoted near the beginning of this book:

> The beginning of wisdom is this: Get wisdom, and whatever you get, get insight. Prize her highly, and she will exalt you; she will honor you if you embrace her.
>
> —PROVERBS 4:7–8

God frequently addresses His people in terms of their self-interests. For example, do you want to not be judged? Then don't judge (Matt. 7:1; Luke 6:37). Do you want to prosper? Then give generously (2 Cor. 9:6). So do you want wisdom? Then fear the Lord. It's free. Yes, it costs—in terms of your self-esteem and things you might have to give up. But it is offered to you, right at your fingertips; begin at once to fear God. And don't look back.

It's a pretty good deal, if you ask me. Though it may cost you all you have, what you get in return exceeds what you gave up a thousand times over. You will live well. Wisdom is the presence of the mind of the Holy Spirit. He knows what to do next. He doesn't make mistakes. He invites you to get in on His infinite, unimprovable, and perfect knowledge. You will soar.

And You will die well. You will finish well. And get more of God in the meantime.

It comes to this: personal discipline. Self-control, a fruit of the Spirit (Gal. 5:22–23), enables you to make a promise and keep it—the promise to read your Bible regularly. Get a Bible-reading plan that will take you through the Bible in a year. As the years fly by, you will be so glad you began reading God's Word daily—at least two, if not four, chapters a day. Personal discipline will enable you to keep your promise to pray more. If you are not a minister or church leader, I recommend praying for at least thirty minutes a day. If you are a minister or church leader, I suggest praying no less than one hour a day.

During my last year at Westminster Chapel, I was invited to address one hundred clergymen in London. I was given ten minutes to speak on the subject of prayer. I used those ten minutes to persuade those ministers to spend no less than one hour a day in prayer. My message was much appreciated.

Daily reading two to four chapters of the Bible takes discipline. Praying thirty minutes or one hour a day takes discipline. In other words, if you want more of God, you will be personally disciplined—and keep it up.

## Physical Exercise

I would even add: be disciplined with your body when it comes to diet and exercise. Over fifteen years ago John Paul Jackson gave me a spontaneous, unsolicited word at our dinner table: "R. T., you will live to a ripe old age. But if you don't get in shape physically, you won't enjoy it" (or words something like that). His words sobered me. I took it seriously. T. R. bought me a diet book, which I read from cover to cover. I began to lose weight. I still weigh myself every day, knowing how easy it is to gain weight!

Steve Strang gave me some exercises, which I have kept up daily for over fifteen years. At his suggestion, I hired a trainer. Today I did twenty-one push-ups. I try to do at least twenty every day. It is my opinion that I would not be able to travel as I do—age eighty-three—had I not listened to John Paul Jackson's caution. Because Paul said, "Bodily exercise profiteth little" (1 Tim. 4:8, KJV), many have dismissed physical exercise as unimportant, assuming Paul was putting it down. Dr. Martyn Lloyd-Jones believed Paul was *encouraging* physical exercise while merely showing that godliness is more important. This understanding lines up with how the NIV renders the verse: "Physical training is of some value, but godliness has value for all things, holding promise for both the present life and the life to come."

So too with being disciplined when it comes to your relationship with God. Depending on how much this means to you, you will pray more, read His Word more, and be sure that you have a genuine fear of God. If you don't *need* this chapter, good! If you need and apply what I have said in this chapter, your life will never be the same again. You will be a happier person—I promise it. You will get more of God—I guarantee it. And you will finish well.

## THE HARDEST PART

Before I close this chapter, I'm afraid there is more to be grasped when it comes to personal discipline. It means waiting and waiting. Then more waiting. It means never giving up, no matter how long the wait.

Patience certainly is not one of my greatest virtues. I even hate waiting for a cup of instant coffee to cool down; I often add an ice cube so I can begin sipping it in seconds. After coming to England, I learned to admire the British manner of waiting in a *queue* (waiting in line). They never complain. It is so embarrassing to watch an American tourist jump the queue in England as she might do in an American supermarket.

Like it or not, getting more of God comes to those who desire it so much that they patiently wait for it. No matter how long it takes. After all, God *always* shows up eventually.

And yet I discover I am not alone in my disdain for waiting when I read certain scriptures:

> How long, O LORD? Will you forget me forever?
> How long will you hide your face from me?
> —PSALM 13:1

> O LORD, how long...shall the wicked exult?
> —PSALM 94:3

> O LORD, how long shall I cry for help, and you will not hear?
> —HABAKKUK 1:2

> They cried out with a loud voice, "O Sovereign Lord, holy and true, how long before you will judge and avenge our blood on those who dwell on the earth?"
> —REVELATION 6:10

177

Then I read verses in the Bible that show God not only is sympathetic with our waiting but knows when to step in:

> I waited patiently for the LORD; he inclined to me and heard my cry.
>
> —PSALM 40:1

> For I will not contend forever, nor will I always be angry; for the spirit would grow faint before me, and the breath of life that I made.
>
> —ISAIAH 57:16

> For he knows our frame, he remembers that we are dust.
>
> —PSALM 103:14

> Abraham, having patiently waited, obtained the promise.
>
> —HEBREWS 6:15

God said long ago, "But from there you will seek the LORD your God and you will find him, if you search after him with all your heart and with all your soul" (Deut. 4:29). "You will seek me and find me, when you seek me with all your heart" (Jer. 29:13).

## THREE MORE ENEMIES

To help us patiently wait, we must overcome three enemies of the flesh: (1) a feeling of entitlement, (2) self-pity, and (3) self-righteousness. This triplet from our weak flesh always rears its ugly head when we wait.

- A feeling of entitlement comes when you have been patient for so long, and you begin to think God owes you something. He doesn't, so get over it.

- Self-pity sneaks in when you think you have waited longer than necessary and begin feeling sorry for yourself. Get over this too; self-pity will invariably lead you nowhere.

- Self-righteousness looms even more after a time of doing the right thing. We are born with it and never get eradicated from it. Never forget how our Lord loathed self-righteousness as exemplified by the Pharisees (Matt. 6:1ff; 23:5ff).

Don't give in to any of these imposters. Ever. I think of Winston Churchill's famous resolve in World War II:

> Never give in, never given in, never, never, never, never—in nothing, great or small, large or petty—never give in except to convictions of honour and good sense. Never yield to force; never yield to the apparently overwhelming might of the enemy.[4]

## LAST BUT NOT LEAST

Our real enemy is the devil. Never forget that. "Resist the devil, and he will flee from you" (Jas. 4:7). His breath is invariably behind a feeling of entitlement, self-pity, and self-righteousness. Know too that the three Rs of spiritual warfare: recognize, refuse, and resist. Learn to *recognize* the devil. Don't take opposition personally, even though people will stand in your way or attempt to bring you down. Recognize who the real enemy is—the devil; your war is not with "flesh and blood"—people (Eph. 6:12). Do not be ignorant of his schemes (2 Cor. 2:11). *Refuse* to listen to him. Don't give his evil suggestions the time of day. Refuse to think about them. Then *resist* him. He will flee from you.

> Your adversary the devil prowls around like a roaring lion, seeking someone to devour. Resist him, firm in your faith, knowing that the same kinds of suffering are being experienced by your brotherhood throughout the world. And after you have suffered a little while, the God of all grace, who has called you to his eternal glory in Christ, will himself restore, confirm, strengthen, and establish you.
>
> —1 PETER 5:8–10

Never, never, never, never give up. The old cliché is absolutely true: God is never too late, never too early, but always right on time.

# Chapter 10

## THE PRAISE THAT COMES FROM GOD

*How can you believe, when you receive
glory from one another and do not seek the
glory that comes from the only God?*
—JOHN 5:44

T HIS IS IT. My final chapter shows *what you get* when God shows up. It reveals what follows, sooner or later, if you genuinely want but also seek more of God.

Here is the irony: by seeking more of God, you end up getting more *from* God after all! By having a desire for more *of* God rather trying to get something *from* Him,

181

there is this surprising bonus: we get something *from* Him. And what is that?

*We get Him.*

This, dear reader, is as good as it gets. In fact, it does not and cannot get better than this. How does that make you feel? If the knowledge that you get *Him* thrills you from head to toe, you are in good shape spiritually. But if you say, "Oh, is that all there is?" I have to tell you as lovingly but firmly as I know how, you sadly show that you only want things *from* Him and His presence is not a priority.

Another way of explaining what you get from Him is a reward. That reward is the praise that comes to you from God. It is worth the wait. His reward is revealed in two stages: (1) in the here and now and (2) at the judgment seat of Christ.

God will show His pleasure with you *here on earth*—at a time when you least expect it. He will ultimately do it once for all at the judgment seat of Christ, when His final verdict will be revealed: "[He] will bring to light the things now hidden in darkness and will disclose the purposes of the heart. Then each one will receive his commendation from God" (1 Cor. 4:5). Jesus spoke about reward at the end of the Book of Revelation.

> Behold, I am coming soon, bringing my recompense
> with me, to repay each one for what he has done.
> —REVELATION 22:12

It's a huge reward. An incalculably rich reward: God's praise. His honor. His glory. The praise of God is His reward for you and me making an effort to obtain His approval as opposed to seeking the praise of people. The principle of losing your life for His sake and then finding it (Matt. 10:39) lies behind this happening. If we chase after what we can get from God, we will probably never get it, but if we make every effort to get more of God, He will reward us with praise, honor, and glory. My advice: adjust your focus on primarily getting all you can *of* God, and He will surprise you by doing "far more abundantly than all that we ask or think" (Eph. 3:20).

Of course you put all your prayer requests to Him! Of course you pray for your loved ones, for good health, healing, financial help, direction, and prosperity! Consider the Lord's Prayer. Jesus worded this pattern prayer in such a way that we would focus *first* on God rather than our-selves when we approach Him.

> Our Father in heaven, hallowed be your name. Your kingdom come, your will be done, on earth as it is in heaven.
>
> —MATTHEW 6:9–10

The Lord's Prayer is a God-centered prayer. We must initially focus on God and His priorities for us. Then we pray for our physical and spiritual needs.

> Give us this day our daily bread, and forgive us our debts, as we also have forgiven our debtors. And lead us not into temptation, but deliver us from evil.
>
> —MATTHEW 6:11–13

The Lord will show up at the time you least expect it. Suddenly, without notice, He comes with His reward.

I've written this final chapter to assure you that all your waiting and praying and dignifying trials is not for nothing! God *will* step in. He *will* come. The writer of Hebrews refers to this twofold coming of the Lord—in the here and now and at the final judgment.

> For, "Yet a little while, and the coming one will come and will not delay."
> —HEBREWS 10:37

## WHAT ABOUT THE HERE AND NOW?

What exactly comes from God in the here and now? Jesus answers, "The glory [praise] that comes from the only God" (John 5:44), as I shall explain.

As some readers might recall, John 5:44 has been my "life verse" for over sixty years. This does not mean I have faithfully carried out this principle for sixty years; I only mean that this has been my *choice of goal* for these years. Jesus does not tell us we must carry this out perfectly; He says we must *attempt* to do it. The Pharisees missed their Messiah because, as Jesus said to them, they "make no effort to obtain" the praise that comes from the only God.

Implied in this crucial verse is that God promises to bless you if you seek His glory rather than man's approval.

## NO GREATER PROMISE CAN BE CONCEIVED

I could make a case that John 5:44 contains the greatest offer in the Bible. Jesus sets forward a covenant promise from the Father that if you will put the praise of God first—and willingly forego the praise of man—He will grant you the highest honor that can be envisaged on this planet. As you read these lines, heaven offers you a pledge that the God of the Bible will grant you a privilege that can only come from Him. What can be greater than the Most High God rewarding you with His honor? Honors such as having dinner with the president, having tea with the queen, winning an Olympic gold medal, or winning a Nobel Peace Prize don't even come close to the privilege offered in John 5:44.

The promise is that praise from the one true God *will come* to you and me. But God bases the offer on a condition: that we will consciously seek His honor and put in abeyance the praise of man. That's the deal. By the way, God would not entice us to seek the honor that comes from Him were there not something in it for us. It is a common thread from Genesis to Revelation: God gets our attention and motivates us by appealing to our self-interest.

And yet some might not be the slightest bit interested in this kind of honor. Some would far prefer to have tea with the queen or receive a Nobel Prize than to have the praise of God. Some people *live* for the praise and approval of people. It's what matters to them. Indeed, it is *all* that matters to them. The praise of God means utterly nothing to most people.

Therefore, this is not an offer that is generally appealing. It is like offering water to someone who is not thirsty, gourmet food to someone who has no appetite, or a cruise around the world to someone who is afraid of water.

Desiring more of God is an ambition most people don't have. But if you, the reader, honestly wish for God's praise more than anything in the world, I have good news: God will honor you for wanting this. He delights to give His praise to those who seek it.

That said, I must add that *not* having this desire and *not* making an effort to seek God's praise has the bleakest of consequences. John 5:44 shows how you can miss the current move of God simply because your appetite is not for more of God. As I said previously, this verse shows how the Israelites missed their Messiah. Jesus wept over the city of Jerusalem because the Israelites forfeited what should have been theirs (Luke 19:41–44). Think about it! It did not cross their minds to desire and seek the glory of God. Think of their great heritage! Abraham, Isaac, Jacob, Moses, Samuel, Elijah, Elisha, and the Old Testament prophets would have in common a longing to honor the true God and seek His glory above the praise of men. That was their background.

But they missed what God was doing in their day by choosing the approval of one another rather than making an effort to seek the praise of the only God. That is exactly how they missed their Messiah. And that is how people can miss what God is doing in a given generation. Jonathan Edwards is often quoted as saying that the task of every generation is to discover in which direction the sovereign Redeemer is moving, and then move in that direction.

The sovereign God of heaven and earth will reveal His praise to you *now*.

Remember, the word *praise* comes from the Greek

word *doxa*—glory. Honor. The root word of *doxa* means opinion. It means His *will*. It is what God wants, what He chooses. It is when God unveils His opinion, the knowledge of His will. God's opinion and God's will are the same thing. The glory of God is the dignity of His will. The praise that comes from Him is the revealing of His will, or opinion.

God has an opinion about everything. When His opinion turns out to be His praise of *you* for seeking His glory over the applause of people, it is a thrill you cannot put into words. There is no greater feeling in this world that the knowledge that we please God.

The question is, How does God *show* us that we please Him? After all, at the judgment seat of Christ, His opinion will be openly revealed before every person who ever lived. But on earth—this side of that fearful event—He will show us His opinion. Yes. Now. That is, if we have sought His honor over the approval of people.

The question therefore is, How does God show His approval of us here on earth? The answer: His presence does it. When He moves in, we know it. It is joy unspeakable and full of glory. It is internal. It is not for the world. It is not for your friends. It is not for your enemies. It is for you. Another way of putting it: it is the immediate and direct witness of the Holy Spirit. When this comes, it is unmistakably recognizable. You know it.

## BEING CONTENT WITH YOUR ROLE

In chapter 4 I emphasized that we must accept our anointing and the limits of it, as in Romans 12:3:

> I say to everyone among you not to think of himself
> more highly than he ought to think, but to think
> with sober judgment, each according to the measure
> of faith that God has assigned.

This means that we should not take ourselves so seriously. I suppose some of us—especially those who have a lot of ambition and like the limelight—will always fight this matter of taking ourselves too seriously. I know that I do. But a great sense of God's immediate presence helps immeasurably here. For example, consider what Paul says about our particular role in the body of Christ. He compares the body of Christ to the human body. He speaks of the head, the eye, the hand—being visible parts of the body, these refer to high profile and prominent responsibility.

> The eye cannot say to the hand, "I have no need of
> you," nor again the head to the feet, "I have no need
> of you." On the contrary, the parts of the body that
> seem to be weaker are indispensable, and on those
> parts of the body that we think less honorable we
> bestow the greater honor, and our unpresentable
> parts are treated with greater modesty, which our
> more presentable parts do not require. But God
> has so composed the body, giving greater honor to
> the part that lacked it, that there may be no divi-
> sion in the body, but that the members may have
> the same care for one another. If one member suf-
> fers, all suffer together; if one member is honored,
> all rejoice together.
> —1 CORINTHIANS 12:21–26

Those parts of the body such as the head or eye would refer to the highest profile in the body of Christ—as apostles, prophets, and teachers. The "unpresentable" parts—such as the kidneys or pancreas—are vital to the body's physical survival. We tend to take them for granted, as those with the gift of "helps" (1 Cor. 12:28, KJV). They don't get noticed.

Paul's application is this: Not all are the eye or head—not all are apostles. Not all have the gift of miracles or teaching. Not everyone can be "up front" and consequently get a lot of attention. Not every servant of Christ can be a Billy Graham. As I said in my book on jealousy, Billy Graham has made more ministers jealous than any figure in church history! Or to bring it closer to home, I have had to accept that I am no Charles Spurgeon or Dr. Martyn Lloyd-Jones.

Here's the point: When the ocean is at low tide, one can see the debris and shells on the seashore. It is like when jealousy creeps in; it can be an unpleasant sight. But when the tide comes in, it covers the debris. When there is a great sense of the presence of God, jealousy diminishes. The result is we are happy to be the pancreas or small intestines and have no profile! The power of the Spirit helps you and me to come to terms with the limit of our faith or place in the kingdom of God.

Paul wants us to think soberly about the measure—or limit—of our anointing whether the tide is in or out. But when the tide comes in, it is a lot easier to accept our place in the body of Christ, whether it be high profile or low profile. The greater the sense of God's presence, the easier it is to accept our limits; the less we experience God's presence, the harder it is to cope with not being recognized or appreciated.

Those who choose the praise, honor, and glory of God rather than the approval of people have this promise: *we will be able to rejoice* in our situation or calling, whatever it be—whether having the gift of "helps" or being an apostle. It is such a good feeling. The reward for seeking the honor and glory of God and not the praise of people is the *inner peace* to accept little or no profile in the body of Christ.

## INCREMENTS OF GLORY IN THE PRESENT LIFE

Sometimes the word *glory* can be defined as an experience. It is something you feel, this being special grace for the moment. It is conscious, momentous, and filled with joy. However, I must repeat what I said earlier: a measure of suffering—I would even call it a satanic attack—frequently precedes the experience of being changed from "glory to glory" (2 Cor. 3:18, KJV).

The conscious praise of God may come to us in increments—often suddenly and unexpectedly. I refer to special touches of the Spirit of God that you can *feel,* increases of the *sense* of His presence. Although this may *appear* to be subjective and appealing to one's emotions, what I am now describing—strange as it may seem—is the opposite of that. It is objectively real. That is, the person who experiences this finds it as real as what he or she sees, smells, tastes, or touches. Others won't see it. That is why one has to say it would appear to be subjective. But to the person who receives this measure of God's presence, it is as real as if seeing with his very eyes.

## DR. D. MARTYN LLOYD-JONES (1899–1981)

One of my predecessors at Westminster Chapel was the great Dr. Martyn Lloyd-Jones. He had a towering intellect. He was a medical doctor, a protégé of King George VI's physician, Lord Horder, but became the greatest preacher of our day—certainly the greatest since C. H. Spurgeon and possibly the greatest ever. Many of his reformed followers, however, are embarrassed by his teaching of the Holy Spirit. And yet it is the key to understanding how his mind worked. Not only did Dr. Lloyd-Jones uphold the teaching that the gifts of the Spirit are available for our day; he was adamant to stress that the witness of the Spirit is something one *feels*. He was unashamed to refer to the witness of the Spirit as an experience. He believed that the baptism of the Holy Spirit—which he also liked to call sealing of the Spirit, as in Ephesians 1:13—was normally *subsequent* to conversion. He quotes John Wesley that the witness of the Holy Spirit is "something immediate and direct, not the result of reflection or argumentation."[1] Dr. Lloyd-Jones believed you could be a good Christian "long before you have this direct witness of the Spirit, this overwhelming experience."[2] He loathed the idea that the baptism of the Holy Spirit was unconscious and stated again and again that it was a conscious experience. I now quote from my book *Holy Fire* (Charisma House):

He believed that the Galatians had experienced this coming of the Spirit subsequent to their conversion. He interprets Galatians 3:2 in this fashion. Paul said, "I would like to learn just one thing from you: Did you receive the Spirit by the works of the law, or by believing what you heard?" The Doctor made this observation: "How can anyone answer that question if this is something outside the realm of experience? How can I know whether I have or have not received the Spirit if it is not something experiential?"[3]

However, this conscious experience after conversion may be but the first of many such experiences of the Holy Spirit. That is why I refer to increments of the Spirit to the believer. It is an immediate and direct witness of the Spirit that may come repeatedly—indeed many, many times.

Such an increment of the Holy Spirit may come while we are actively and consciously praying. It may happen while you are walking in the park or down the main street in town. It could come while you are in a shopping mall. It may occur when you are reading the Bible—any part of it. It may come when you are singing a song or a hymn. It may happen as you are driving, walking to work, chatting or texting with someone, or reaching for a book or newspaper. It could come while you are watching television or posting something on social media. It may occur just before you go to sleep. It may come when you first wake up; indeed, this increment of glory could even wake you up!

When D. L. Moody (1837–1899) first experienced it, he

was in New York. It was so powerful that Moody asked God to "stay His hand."[4]

## A HIGH LEVEL OF ASSURANCE

An increment of glory—being changed from one level of glory to another—always means a dose of greater assurance. It is when God comes unmistakably. God knows what we need at that moment. I am talking about touches from God that can certainly affect your emotions. But it is objective. You know it. You feel it. The Greek word is *plerophoria*, meaning full or complete assurance. You can apply it in more than one way. Here are some examples of what having more of God will do for you:

1. It will give you full assurance of hope. *Plerophoria* is used to describe full assurance of "hope"—when it is as though what you were waiting for has already come (Heb. 6:11–13), or as when Jesus said, "Believe that you have received it, and it will be yours" (Mark 11:24).

2. It will make God very, very real to you; it is what happens when God swears an oath to you, as we will see further in the pages to come.

3. You have the conscious faith to accept things *as they are* without grumbling.

4. The need to try to make things happen and nudge the arm of providence diminishes;

you remember that only God can change the water into wine.

5. You may receive full assurance of understanding (Col. 2:2), as when a doctrinal issue or a particular Bible verse becomes crystal clear. To people for whom doctrinal aptness and accuracy are very important, this is one of the greatest things that happen as a sign of God's praise.

6. The willingness to let God vindicate you becomes easy, as when David did not want to take advantage of the ark of the covenant in his exile but waited for God to bring him back to Jerusalem (2 Sam. 15:25).

7. True wisdom sets in—having the presence of the mind of the Holy Spirit. Such assurance lies behind God showing the next step forward to know His will. Wisdom may be defined as knowing what to do next. Full assurance by the Spirit can make this clear to us.

8. You'll experience a feeling of being expendable. It is the polar opposite of taking oneself too seriously or having a feeling of entitlement. Paul did not count his life dear; "I do not account my life of any value nor as precious to myself" (Acts 20:24); those who overcame Satan by the blood of

the Lamb "loved not their lives even unto death" (Rev. 12:11).

9. You'll accept your anointing and the limit of it (Rom. 12:3)—and not complain that you are not as able or gifted as someone else.

10. You will experience a spontaneous flow of the "fruit of the Spirit," as in Galatians 5:22–23; the increment of glory will bring joy and supernatural peace.

It is often a baptism of *agape* love—unselfish love—when the love of God may actually make total forgiveness an experience without having to exercise your will! It is when a feeling of overwhelming love makes forgiving someone as easy as eating blackberry cobbler. Whereas total forgiveness is normally an act of the will, when the Holy Spirit comes in great power, the love described in 1 Corinthians 13 may manifest without any effort! That, however, may not always come with an increase of His glory. Mind you, as I shall show further, any increment of glory is temporary. You will need a refill—another increment of glory. But at the moment, it is almost overwhelming and certainly unforgettable.

## WHEN GOD SWEARS AN OATH TO YOU

Hebrews 6:18 refers to *two* immutable, or unchangeable, things—namely, the promise and the oath. Both are from God; both are equally true and reliable. But a promise is normally given to us on condition—often containing an *if*.

It is when God says, "I will do this if you will do that." A famous verse is 2 Chronicles 7:14:

> If my people who are called by my name humble themselves, and pray and seek my face and turn from their wicked ways, then I will hear from heaven and will forgive their sin and heal their land.

And yet John 5:44 is also a promise. The word *if* is not explicit but is assumed; the praise that comes from God is promised to those who choose God's approval over that of people.

However, I must say more: John 5:44 is the promise of the *oath*. One way you know you have been given the praise of God is that he confirms the promise by an oath. The main thing about the oath is that it removes all doubts. And yet sometimes God renews His promises before He swears the oath to us. He might even give a succession of promises. He did this with Abraham. It was promise after promise (Gen. 12:2, 7; 13:15–17; 15:5; 17:6–8, 15–16; 18:14, 27–32). Promises, promises.

But one day God swore an oath to Abraham, which turned out to be the crowning experience of his life. The writer of Hebrews refers to this oath. Do not forget that both the promise and the oath are equally reliable and equally true since both are given by the same God who cannot lie (Heb. 6:18).

But when an oath is given, there are no remaining conditions, delays, or doubts. The oath is always very real, very clear, and totally persuasive. It "is final for confirmation" (Heb. 6:16). If you have to ask, "Have I received an oath?"

almost certainly you haven't. You know it is an oath when God Himself has overruled, intervened, stepped in, and made Himself very, very real.

To summarize: an oath is supernatural, unmistakable, and utterly convincing. For example, an oath is so clear it bypasses the need to reason your way to assurance. Not that there is anything wrong with using reason. It is perfectly legitimate and biblical to say, "I know I am saved because I have trusted Jesus Christ." That is a valid way of coming to assurance of salvation. But when God swears an oath to you, you do not have to reason your way to assurance. The immediate witness of the Spirit does it for you. You feel it. You know it. The swearing of an oath is what happened when God swore to Abraham after he became willing to sacrifice Isaac.

> By myself I have sworn, declares the LORD, because you have done this and have not withheld your son, your only son, I will surely bless you, and I will surely multiply your offspring as the stars of heaven and as the sand that is on the seashore.
>
> —GENESIS 22:16–17

Abraham received this oath after waiting patiently. He was around eighty-five years old when he received the promise that led to his being credited with righteousness.

> And behold, the word of the LORD came to [Abraham]: "This man [Eliezer] shall not be your heir; your very own son shall be your heir." And [God] brought [Abraham] outside and said, "Look

toward heaven, and number the stars, if you are able to number them." Then [God] said to him, "So shall your offspring be."

—Genesis 15:4–5

That was the *promise*. Abraham believed it. He might have said, "God, You cannot be serious. Don't tease me. Do You expect me to believe a word like that?"

But no, Abraham believed that promise, and God "counted it to him as righteousness" (Gen. 15:6). That became the biblical foundation for Paul's teaching of justification by faith alone (Rom. 4:1–5). That, as I said, came to Abraham when he was eighty-five. And yet it was approximately twenty years later—at age 105—that God swore the oath to him.

This is what the writer means by the words "Abraham, having patiently waited, obtained the promise" (Heb. 6:15)—namely, the oath. Note carefully: "obtained the promise." Abraham was promised descendants as numerous as the stars in the heavens and the sand on the seashore. However, could Abraham *see* his offspring? This would take hundreds and hundreds of years! How could he see countless generations of peoples to come that would be so numerous that "no one could number" (Rev. 7:9)? The answer: the oath did it. The oath was so real that the countless billions were as good as born and born again! That was how real the oath was to Abraham. He would no longer have to "exercise faith," as it were; the oath was the equivalent to the reality.

The first noticeable ingredient in an oath is *how real*

*God is. How true His Word is.* It will enable you to believe that the Bible is infallible. It is not as though an oath replaces the need for faith. But it is *almost* like that. Whereas faith is being convinced of what you do not see (Heb. 11:1), an oath puts an end to the argument. No more need for reasoning. It is an increment of glory.

## WHY RENEWAL AFTER RECEIVING AN OATH?

You may say, "Then why be changed from one level of glory to another if you have once received an oath?" The answer: "Even an oath needs to be renewed with further increments of glory from the throne of grace." We are all human. We remain human. We have the devil as an enemy. No increment of glory this side of heaven permanently removes the need for further "times of refreshing" from the Lord (Acts 3:20). Even after Pentecost, the disciples received another outpouring of the Spirit that shook the place and filled them again (Acts 4:31).

The most delicious food that fills you up does not keep you from being hungry again. The sweetest and coolest water you drink does not keep you from being thirsty again. So an oath needs to be followed with increments of glory that make God more and more real. The more of God you receive, the more of God you want.

That said, once the oath has initially been sworn to you, it is a peak experience. It is an experience that you can never forget, possibly like the disciples seeing the transfiguration of Jesus (Matt. 17:1–8). They would need more teaching and more encouragement. But they would never forget seeing Jesus transfigured before their eyes. In the same way once an oath is given, you can never doubt that moment and what it meant to you. But after a while, you want more. And more.

## OTHERS SEEING JESUS IN US

I cannot avoid this part of the book. But I find it painful. Paul speaks of "Christ in you, the hope of glory" (Col. 1:27). Paul prayed for the Ephesians "that Christ may dwell in your hearts through faith" (Eph. 3:17). It is one thing to experience His presence and quite another for others to see Christ in us.

In other words, if Christ is in us, should not people *see Him* when they look at us?

I have to admit to you that I feel the least qualified to write this part of my book. I do so want others to see Jesus in me. If only. I have a pretty shrewd suspicion what people see in me—or how they perceive me: an old man with perhaps a bit of wisdom, a theologian, a Bible teacher. That's it. I fear they don't see Jesus—only a teacher. I would like to think that God is not finished with me yet and that He would be merciful to an old man and grant a Christlikeness that is long overdue.

I think of Arthur Blessitt. An Arab sheikh saw Arthur in a restaurant in Amman, Jordan, and insisted on paying his bill—all because of watching Arthur at a distance. When Arthur asked why the sheikh paid his bill, the Arab looked at him and said, "I want what you've got." Arthur asked what he meant. The Arab sheikh replied, "Look at all these people. No one is smiling. But you have a smile, a glow on your face. I want what you've got." Arthur then explained that he was a follower of Jesus Christ, who died on the cross for our sins. Arthur afterward presented the gospel to him and then led the Arab sheikh to pray to receive Jesus.

Christ in us may bring an inward joy; there is no doubt about that. But it should also be visible to others.

## VINDICATION

Vindication means having your name cleared from doubt, blame, or suspicion. It is a very satisfying experience, especially if those you love have doubted you, or if those who admire you were shaken by what was purported to be true about you—but was not true. The need to be vindicated can run very deep, and it can be very painful and intrusive; it can be hard to think of anything else when you have been falsely accused or misunderstood.

But here's the deal: *vindication is what God does.* Like its twin, vengeance, it is the Lord's prerogative to punish those who have hurt you (Deut. 32:35; Rom. 12:19; Heb. 10:30). God does not like it one bit when you or I lift a finger to vindicate ourselves. He doesn't want our help, nor does He need it.

Here is a guarantee: start trying to clear your name, and watch God distance Himself from you. If you get personally involved in the matter of vindicating yourself, you will find that God removes Himself from doing it. He wants to do it all by Himself. And by the way, *how* He does it is not only "past finding out" (Rom. 11:33, KJV); it is a more beautiful and thrilling picture than you or I could come up with even if we had a thousand years to plan it.

201

Like a master artist who does not need anyone's touch of the brush, so the master vindicator will complete the painting with style, elegance, and awe that will take your breath away. In a word, don't deprive God of doing what He *loves* to do.

## TWO KINDS OF VINDICATION

There are two kinds of vindication: (1) internal—the witness of the Spirit, and (2) external—what is visible to everyone. The latter is what we naturally want first. But it is the internal vindication you should seek after; it is the same as seeking His praise in John 5:44. God may or may not give you external vindication in this life; it is only guaranteed at the judgment seat of Christ. But the internal vindication is what you can surely have; it is the same as when God swears an oath to you.

When God swears an oath, it refers to internal vindication—utterly persuasive and satisfying. That is what Abraham got.

You may say, "When God openly vindicates for all to see, it is certainly very satisfying." Agreed. But it is also a fleshly experience. It requires no faith. It is like a compliment; we all love them. It is a pat on the back. And sometimes God is pleased to give you the praise of people—even as a sign of His praise. But don't look for it, and never seek it.

One more thing: God only vindicates the truth. It is not *you* who gets vindicated but the truth. Whether what you believe is doctrinally pure and sound. The truth of what you did or said. The truth of what they did or said. The truth will come out—like it or not: "Nothing is hidden that will not be made manifest, nor is anything secret that will not be known and come to light" (Luke 8:17).

Jesus' vindication was internal. He was "vindicated by the Spirit" (1 Tim. 3:16). He did *not* receive His joy from the crowds, His disciples, or their praise. He always looked to the Father. Always.

> Truly, truly, I say to you, the Son can do nothing of his own accord, but only what he sees the Father doing. For whatever the Father does, that the Son does likewise....I do not receive glory from people....I do nothing on my own authority, but speak just as the Father taught me....I always do the things that are pleasing to him.
>
> —JOHN 5:19, 41; 8:28–29

Jesus got His joy from the Spirit's witness. The Holy Spirit told Him that He pleased the Father. That is what Jesus cared about. Everything He did was to please the Father. Everything the Pharisees did was for men to see (Matt. 23:5). But the internal vindication by the Spirit motivated Jesus.

In other words, Jesus did not need the Pharisees' approval. He did not even want it. They were not His people in the first place. Jesus knew that the Pharisees did not believe in Him. But neither had they been given to Him by the Father; they were not among God's chosen. He said to them, "The reason why you do not hear them is that you are not of God" (John 8:47). "You have seen me," Jesus said to the Pharisees, "and yet do not believe." But not to worry! "All that *the Father gives me will* come to me" (John 6:36–37, emphasis added). It is Jesus' way of saying, be it ever so sharply: "You Pharisees do not believe in Me because God did not choose you. But those He chose *will* believe in Me." Strong words. "A hard saying," said many of His disciples (John 6:60). "This is why I told you that no one can come to me unless it is granted him by the Father," Jesus concluded (John 6:65; cf. 6:44).

Jesus was never vindicated by the crowds. He was not vindicated by the Jews, the chief priest, Herod, or Pilate. His vindication was by the Spirit. God's oath to His Son was a nonstop, ongoing revelation. It is the way Jesus got His joy and affirmation. At His baptism, the Father said, "This is my beloved Son, with whom I am well pleased" (Matt. 3:17). When He was transfigured before the disciples, the Father said, "This is my beloved Son, with whom I am well pleased; listen to him" (Matt. 17:5).

## OUTWARD VINDICATION IS NOT PROMISED IN THIS LIFE

Jesus must be our role model. We too must get our vindication by the Holy Spirit: the internal testimony, the immediate and direct witness, the oath sworn to us that we please God.

I'm sorry, but outward vindication is not promised in this life. We might want it more than anything. We might crave it. We might plead with God to grant it. We might go on a fast to obtain it. But God never promised that vengeance, vindication, or proof of the Father's approval would be openly seen by our friends, loved ones, or enemies in this present life. God could do that, of course. And sometimes He does! But it is not promised. So don't count on it.

In one of my bleakest moments I opened my Bible, and my eyes fell on these words:

> This is evidence of the righteous judgment of God, that you may be considered worthy of the kingdom of God, for which you are also suffering—since indeed God considers it just to repay with affliction those who afflict you, and to grant relief to you who are afflicted as well as to us...
>
> —2 THESSALONIANS 1:5–7

"Oh, good!" I thought. "Wow. This is wonderful." That is, until I kept reading...

> ...when the Lord Jesus is revealed from heaven with his mighty angels.
>
> —2 THESSALONIANS 1:7

Oh no! Oh dear. Must I wait that long? Yes, I'm afraid so.

It is true that God can and sometimes does vindicate and even bring vengeance on those who have hurt us here below. Sometimes.

But don't count on the external vindication until the judgment seat of Christ. You may or may not get it then! Why do I say this? Because there is the possibility that you don't have vindication coming to you after all! One thing is sure: you will find out when God's final judgment reveals the truth (1 Cor. 4:5). God *vindicates the truth*. When the truth is revealed—and you have vindication coming—you will get it. In any case God will have the last word. It will be worth the wait.

## THE JUDGMENT SEAT OF CHRIST

> For we must all appear before the judgment seat of Christ, so that each one may receive what is due for what he has done in the body, whether good or evil.
> —2 CORINTHIANS 5:10

The ultimate joy that will come to those who sought more of God on earth will take place at the judgment seat of Christ. This is a translation of the word *bema*—the bema seat being the place where rewards and punishments were handed out in ancient Corinth. Paul uses a word that the Corinthians would have fully understood. Those believers who truly wanted *and* sought more of God on earth—"in the body"—will be rewarded at the judgment seat of Christ with the greatest conceivable "congratulations." This will come from the lips of Jesus Himself.

I agree with those who say, "Surely having more of God while in the body is a reward in itself." I would also say that totally forgiving others is its own reward; indeed, love is its own reward. But there is still even more reward later. Those who forgave, prayed for, and blessed their enemies will have a great reward in heaven (Luke 6:35), said Jesus. Paul says so too. "If the work that anyone has built on the foundation survives, he will receive a reward" (1 Cor. 3:14). Those, therefore, who wanted more of God get a double blessing: (1) the immediate presence of God while in the body, plus (2) the reward at the judgment seat of Christ.

Such people received only a finite measure of God's sense of approval on earth. Being changed from "glory to glory" does not compare with what is coming. The apostle Paul said,

> For I consider that the sufferings of this present time are not worth comparing with the glory that is to be revealed to us.
>
> —ROMANS 8:18

But God saves the best for last. This will be seen at the judgment seat of Christ.

I will not enter into the chronological and eschatological details that surround this fearful event, nor will I deal with God's judgment of the wicked—those who are forever lost—in this book. What Paul refers to in 1 Corinthians 3:12–15 and 2 Corinthians 5:10 is the *Christians'* judgment. *All of the saved* will stand before Christ's judgment seat. The judge is Jesus Christ Himself (Acts 17:31). It will follow His second coming (2 Tim. 4:1; Heb. 9:27–28). Paul calls Jesus "the righteous judge" (2 Tim. 4:8). The verdict will be righteous. Fair. Just. Final. What a contrast to judges on this earth who can be bribed, threatened, and influenced by favor, and who let people get away with murder and endless corruption. But not at the judgment seat of Christ.

This is the day of days that God's prophets have forecast for centuries. It is called "a day against all that is proud and lofty" (Isa. 2:12), "the day of the LORD" (Amos 5:18), and the "great and awesome day of the LORD" (Joel 2:31). Although Jesus had not touched on the final judgment in the Sermon on the Mount, there was so much awareness of this day that He only needed to refer to "that day" when He approached the end of His sermon. "On that day many will say to me, 'Lord, Lord, did we not prophesy in your name?'" (Matt. 7:22). Everyone knew what that day was.

On that day of days, then, we will witness the ultimate and final verdict from the Most High God—the God of perfect justice. For some it will be the scariest day that ever was. It will be more fearful on that day than the day God revealed the Law—when Moses trembled at the sight (Heb. 12:21). Anxiety in the hearts of those who did not want more of God will reach a peak beyond any level experienced before. It is when all men and women will have to give an account of every careless word they have spoken (Matt. 12:36). It is when the Christian will receive his or her reward. It is when the truth about everything and everybody will be out in the open.

But with one glorious exception: sins repented of and washed away by the blood of Jesus will not come up.

If we have pursued our inheritance faithfully while "in the body"—demonstrating that we wanted more of God— we will receive a reward. In other words, if we erected the previously mentioned superstructure of gold, silver, and precious gems while "in the body" we will receive a reward. Paul says the day will be "revealed by fire" (1 Cor. 3:13), that the fire will test the quality of everyone's work. Whether that fire is literal or metaphorical—or maybe both—I don't know for sure.

I will not speculate as to what this reward will look like or what it will be. I am satisfied that it is God's "well done." That is good enough for me.

If we erected a superstructure of wood, hay, or straw, we will be saved by fire but receive no reward (1 Cor. 3:12–15). I cannot fathom how painful this will be for those who are saved by fire.

The reward to be given is the ultimate praise from the only God. This is when the promise of John 5:44—namely, that those who eschewed honor from men but chose the honor and praise that comes from the only God—will be experienced.

On earth that praise was in increments—mere touches of His sense of approval. But at the judgment seat of Christ one will receive the ultimate praise of God. For those who built their superstructure with gold, silver, and precious stones but who went to heaven prior to this final judgment "there will be richly provided for [them] an entrance" (2 Pet. 1:11). But the final reward will be meted out at the judgment seat of Christ.

I cannot imagine what it will be like. John talks about having "confidence" on the day of judgment (1 John 2:28; 4:17) The King James Version says "boldness" (1 John 4:17). That would surely apply to those who have faithfully walked in the light in their earthly journey (1 John 1:7).

The central theme throughout the day of judgment will be *vindication*. It will be vindication for God—that is, how He could be seen in the Bible as a God of mercy and justice and allow evil at the same time and still be just. God will clear His name (Hab. 2:1–4). Please see my book *Totally Forgiving God*, in which I explain how the prophet Habakkuk grasped this. It will be vindication for the truth—that the Bible is God's infallible Word (John

12:48). It will be vindication for the Lord Jesus Christ—the God-man, that He always was the truth and the only way to the Father (John 14:6; Phil. 2:9–11). The truth and error of all doctrines held by many people over the centuries will be revealed.

It will be vindication for those who have suffered disdain, false accusations, deep hurt, and gross miscarriages of justice. I cannot imagine what this will be like. How God will expose the bad behavior of some people who were truly saved—and whose sins are forgiven—is a matter I will leave to God. It probably pertains to the superstructure of wood and hay, when those who were saved but vengeful, unforgiving, and ungrateful will somehow be exposed. But I am beginning to speculate!

I know this: God loves to vindicate His Word. He will do this on that final day, and it will be worth the wait. God saves the best for last.

I look forward to it. It also scares me to death.

May the grace of God Almighty—Father, Son, and Holy Spirit—be yours now and evermore. Amen.

# Notes

## CHAPTER 1
### MORE FROM GOD OR MORE OF GOD?

1.    Rolfe Barnard, "Your God vs. the Bible's God," sermon, Ashland, Kentucky, September 29, 1964, https://www.sermonaudio.com/sermoninfo.asp?SID=622121652232.

2.    "O Thou Good omnipotent, who so carest for every one of us, as if Thou caredst for him only; and so for all, as if they were but one!" Saint Augustine, *The Confessions of Saint Augustine*, trans. E. B. Pusey (Gutenberg Project, June 2002), https://www.gutenberg.org/files/3296/3296-h/3296-h.htm.

## CHAPTER 2
### MORE ABOUT GOD OR MORE OF GOD?

1.    Bernard of Clairvaux, "Jesus, the Very Thought of Thee," trans. Edward Caswall, Hymntime.com, accessed August 1, 2018, http://www.hymntime.com/tch/htm/j/t/v/jtveryth.htm.

2.    Eliza E. Hewitt, "More About Jesus," 1887, Timeless Truths, accessed September 19, 2018, https://library.timelesstruths.org/music/More_About_Jesus/.

3.    A. Katherine Hankey, "I Love to Tell the Story," 1866, Hymntime.com, accessed September 19, 2018, http://www.hymntime.com/tch/htm/i/l/t/iltts.htm.

4.    A. Katherine Hankey, "Tell Me the Old, Old Story," 1866, Hymntime.com, accessed September 19, 2018, http://www.hymntime.com/tch/htm/t/e/l/l/tellmoos.htm.

5.    PassItOn.com, s.v. "Andrew Bennett," accessed September 19, 2018, https://www.passiton.com/inspirational-quotes/6679-the-longest-journey-you-will-ever-take-is-the.

6.     Blue Letter Bible, s.v. *"makarios,"* accessed August 3, 2018, https://www.blueletterbible.org/lang/lexicon/lexicon.cfm?Strongs=G3107&t=KJV.

## CHAPTER 3
### OUR NEVER-CHANGING PRIORITY

1.     Grace Quotes, s.v. "Jonathan Edwards," accessed September 19, 2018, https://gracequotes.org/author-quote/jonathan-edwards/.
2.     "John Lennon Sparks His First Major Controversy," A&E Television Networks LLC, accessed August 3, 2018, https://www.history.com/this-day-in-history/john-lennon-sparks-his-first-major-controversy.

## CHAPTER 4
### ACCEPTING OUR LIMITATIONS

1.     John Calvin, *Institutes of the Christian Religion*, ed. John T. McNeill (Louisville, KY: Westminster John Knox Press, 2006), https://books.google.com/books?id=0aB1BwAAQBAJ&pg.
2.     Augustine, *The Confessions of Saint Augustine.*
3.     Richard Baxter, "Ye Holy Angels Bright," accessed August 2, 2018, https://hymnary.org/hymn/CAH2000/755.

## CHAPTER 5
### THE GLORY

1.     William M. Greathouse, *The Fullness of the Spirit* (Kansas City, MO: Nazarene Publishing House, 1958), https://www.whdl.org/sites/default/files/publications/THE%20FULLNESS%20OF%20THE%20SPIRIT.pdf.
2.     "He Sees All You Do," accessed August 2, 2018, https://hymnary.org/text/he_sees_all_you_do#instances.

## CHAPTER 6
### THE SUPERSTRUCTURE

1.     William Martin, *A Prophet With Honor: The Billy Graham Story* (Grand Rapids, MI: Zondervan, 2018), 36, https://www.amazon.com/Prophet-Honor-Billy-Graham-Story/dp/B004HOV0CW.

2.   *Ohio Archaeological and Historical Publications*, vol.
12 (Columbus, OH: Ohio Archaeological and Historical Society,
1903), 244–251, https://books.google.com/books?id
=pj8-AQAAMAAJ&pg.

3.   "God in America—People & Ideas: James Finley," WGBH
Educational Foundation, accessed October 10, 2018, http://www.
pbs.org/godinamerica/people/james-finley.html.

4.   Dallas Bogan, "History of Campbell County,
Tennessee," TNGenNet, accessed October 10, 2018, https://www
.tngenweb.org/campbell/hist-bogan/bible.html.

5.   "God uses lust to impel men to marriage, ambition to
office, avarice to earning, and fear to faith." Quoted in Roland
H. Bainton, *Here I Stand: A Life of Martin Luther* (Nashville:
Abingdon Press, 1978), 302, https://books.google.com
/books?id=thoxAAAAQBAJ&q.

6.   As quoted in Warren W. Wiersbe, *The Wiersbe Bible
Commentary: New Testament* (Colorado Springs, CO: David
C. Cook, 2007), 632, https://books.google.com
/books?id=Sn18qwyJw9QC&pg.

7.   *Luther's Works: Word and Sacrament I*, vol. 35
(Philadelphia: Fortress, 1960), 395–397.

8.   Jenn, "8 Types of Gossip, 26 Bible Verses," *Going by
Faith* (blog), May 2, 2012, http://goingbyfaith.com/types-of
-gossip/.

CHAPTER 7

DIGNIFYING THE TRIAL

1.   Frances R. Havergal, "Like a River Glorious," Hymnary
.org, 1874, https://hymnary.org/hymn/HTLG2017/page/251.

2.   Blue Letter Bible, s.v. *"peirasmos,"* accessed October 15,
2018, https://www.blueletterbible.org/lang/lexicon/lexicon
.cfm?t=kjv&strongs=g3986.

3.   Blue Letter Bible, s.v. *"parapiptō,"* accessed October 15,
2018, https://www.blueletterbible.org/lang/lexicon/lexicon
.cfm?t=kjv&strongs=g3895.

4.   "How Firm a Foundation," Hymnary.org, 1787,
https://hymnary.org/hymn/LSB2006/728.

## Chapter 8
### Total Forgiveness

1.     John F. Kennedy, *The Uncommon Wisdom of JFK*, ed. Bill Adler (New York: Rugged Land, 2003), 194, https://books.google.com/books?id=ko93AAAAMAAJ&dq =the+uncommon+wisdom+of+jfk&focus=searchwithinvolume&q =forgive+your+enemies.

## Chapter 9
### Personal Discipline

1.     Michael W. Chapman, "Rev. Graham: Secularists Are 'Anti-Christ' and 'They've Taken Control of Washington,'" CNSNews.com (blog), January 30, 2015, https://www.cnsnews .com/blog/michael-w-chapman/rev-graham-secularists-are -anti-christ-and-they-ve-taken-control-washington,

2.     William Walford, "Sweet Hour of Prayer," Hymnary.org, 1845, https://hymnary.org/hymn/BH2008/page/590.

3.     As quoted in Roy B. Zuck, *The Speaker's Quote Book* (Grand Rapids, MI: Kregel Publications, 2009).

4.     Winston Churchill, "Never Give In, Never, Never, Never, 1941," National Churchill Museum, October 29, 1941, https:// www.nationalchurchillmuseum.org/never-give-in -never-never-never.html.

## Chapter 10
### The Praise That Comes From God

1.     *The Christian Library*, vol. 3–4 (New York: Thomas George Jr., 1835), 51, https://books.google.com /books?id=aOkWAQAAIAAJ&pg.

2.     D. Martyn Lloyd-Jones, *God's Ultimate Purpose: An Exposition of Ephesians 1* (Grand Rapids, MI: Baker Books, 1978), 275.

3.     R. T. Kendall, *Holy Fire* (Lake Mary, FL: Charisma House, 2014) 46–47; Lloyd-Jones, *God's Ultimate Purpose*, 271.

4.     W. R. Moody, *The Life of Dwight L. Moody* (New York: Fleming H. Revell, 1900), 149, https://www.amazon.com /Life-Dwight-L-Moody/dp/0916441156.